Sir John Summerson
is the acknowledged leader of
English architectural historians. Curator of Sir John
Soane's Museum from 1945 until his retirement in 1984,
he has been Slade Professor of Fine Art at both Oxford
and Cambridge, and has lectured on the history of
architecture at Birkbeck College, London. Of his many
books, the best known are probably *Georgian
London* and *Architecture in Britain 1530–1830*,
both standard works.

# WORLD OF ART

This famous series
provides the widest available
range of illustrated books on art in all its aspects.
If you would like to receive a complete list
of titles in print please write to:
THAMES AND HUDSON
30 Bloomsbury Street, London WC1B 3QP
In the United States please write to:
THAMES AND HUDSON INC.
500 Fifth Avenue, New York, New York 10110

Printed in Singapore

Toscana
parti
.VI.

Dorica
parti
.VII.

Ionica
parti
.VIII.

Coriniba
parti
IX

Compoſi
ta
parti
.X.

Proportione
quadrata

Proportione
diagonea

Proportione
ſeſqui
altero

Proportione
ſuperbipartiens
tertias,

Proportione
dupla

John Summerson

# THE CLASSICAL
# LANGUAGE
# OF ARCHITECTURE

139 illustrations

Thames and Hudson

*Frontispiece:*
**I** The orders of architecture. With this
woodcut of 1540, Sebastiano Serlio
introduced his treatise on 'the five ways of
building'. The Tuscan, Doric, Ionic and
Corinthian orders had been named by
Vitruvius. Alberti had named the Composite.
Serlio was the first to exhibit the five orders
as a closed series to which no additions were
admissible.

*Printed and bound in Singapore by C.S. Graphics*

# Contents

# Preface

This book originated in a series of six talks broadcast by the BBC in 1963, and the text consists of the six scripts, almost unaltered. I make no apology for this because the pleasure I took in preparing the scripts seems to me inseparable from the pleasure I hope to communicate in the subject. Any conventionalizing of the broadcast idiom would be pure loss. One alteration, however, I have been obliged to make. In the broadcasts and the first edition of the book, the history of the classical language was made to fade rather ambiguously into that of the Modern Movement. In recent years, attitudes towards that movement, its nature and principles, and indeed towards the whole trend of architectural development, have profoundly changed and of these changes some account has been taken in paragraphs added to the final chapter.

As an accompaniment to the original series of broadcasts the BBC published an illustrated booklet. The illustrations it contained are all reproduced here and to these have been added nearly sixty more, serving to convey something of the depth, variety and richness of the subject.

J.S.

*Sir John Soane's Museum, September 1979*

# CHAPTER ONE

# The Essentials of Classicism

I must begin by assuming some general knowledge. Like, for instance, knowing that St Paul's Cathedral is a classical building while Westminster Abbey is not; that the British Museum is a classical building while the Natural History Museum at South Kensington is not. That all the buildings round Trafalgar Square – the National Gallery, St Martin-in-the-Fields, Canada House and even (just) South Africa House are classical, that all the public buildings in Whitehall are classical; but that the Houses of Parliament are not. Elementary distinctions, and you may think at once that I am going to deal in superficialities. When is a classical building not a classical building? Does it really matter? Are not the important qualities of architecture deeper than and independent of such stylistic nomenclature? They are. Nevertheless, I cannot reach all the things I want to say in this book without first isolating all the buildings which are, *prima facie*, classical from all the others. I shall be talking about architecture as a language and all I want to assume at the moment is that you do recognize the Latin of architecture when you see it.

The *Latin* of Architecture – that brings me to another general knowledge assumption. Classical architecture has its roots in antiquity, in the worlds of Greece and Rome, in the temple architecture of the Greek world and in the religious, military and civil architecture of the Romans. But this book is not primarily going to be about the architecture of Greece and Rome: it is not going to be about the growth and development of the classical language of architecture but about its nature and its use – its use as the common architectural language, inherited from Rome, of nearly the whole civilized world in the five centuries between the Renaissance and our own time.

Very well – from now on we can be more precise. Let us look at this word 'classical' as applied to architecture. It is a mistake to try to define classicism. It has all sorts of useful meanings in different contexts and I propose to consider two meanings only, both of which will be useful throughout the book. The first meaning is the most

7

obvious. A classical building is one whose decorative elements derive directly or indirectly from the architectural vocabulary of the ancient world – the 'classical' world as it is often called: these elements are easily recognizable, as for example columns of five standard varieties, applied in standard ways; standard ways of treating door and window openings and gable-ends and standard runs of mouldings applicable to all these things.

That, I think, is one fair description of what classical architecture is, but it is only skin-deep; it enables you to recognize the 'uniform' worn by a certain category of buildings, the category we call classical. But it tells you nothing about the essence of classicism in architecture. Here, however, we have got to be rather careful. 'Essences' are very elusive and are often found, on enquiry, not to exist. Nevertheless, embedded in the history of classical architecture is a series of statements about the essentials of architecture and these are in agreement over a long period, to the extent that we may say that the aim of classical architecture has always been to achieve a demonstrable harmony of parts. Such harmony has been felt to reside in the buildings of antiquity and to be to a great extent 'built in' to the principal antique elements – especially to the five 'orders' to which we shall come presently. But it has also been considered in the abstract by a series of theoreticians who have demonstrated that harmony analogous to musical harmony in a structure is achieved by proportion, that is to say by ensuring that the ratios in a building are simple arithmetical functions and that the ratios of all parts of the building are either those same ratios or related to them in a direct way. A vast amount of pretentious nonsense has been written about proportion and I have no intention of getting involved in it. The Renaissance concept of proportion is fairly simple. The purpose of proportion is to establish harmony throughout a structure – a harmony which is made comprehensible either by the conspicuous use of one or more of the orders as dominant components or else simply by the use of dimensions involving the repetition of simple ratios. That is enough for us to go on with.

There is, however, one point about this rather abstract conception of what is classical and it may be put as a question. Is it possible, you may ask, for a building to display absolutely none of the trappings associated with classical architecture and still, by virtue of proportion alone, to qualify as a 'classical' building? The answer must, I think, be 'no'. You can say, in describing such a building, that its proportions are classical, but it is simply confusing and an abuse of terminology to say that it *is* classical. The porches of Chartres Cathedral are, in distribution and proportion, just about as classical as you can get, but nobody is ever going to call them anything but Gothic. And one could cite plenty of other examples of the Gothic system being closely analogous to the classical. It is, by the way, a great mistake to think of Gothic and classical as *opposites*; they are very different but they are not opposites and they are not wholly unrelated. It is nineteenth-century romanticism which has made us put them in totally different psychological camps. People who say they 'prefer' Gothic to classical or classical to Gothic are, I suspect, usually the victims of this nineteenth-century misinterpretation. The fact is that the essentials of architecture – as expounded by the Renaissance theorists – are to be found expressed, consciously or unconsciously, throughout the architectures of the world. And while we must incorporate these essentials in our idea of what is classical we must also accept the fact that classical architecture is only recognizable as such when it contains some allusion, however slight, however vestigial, to the antique 'orders'. Such an allusion may be no more than some groove or projection which suggests the idea of a cornice or even a disposition of windows which suggests the ratio of pedestal to column, column to entablature. Some twentieth-century buildings – notably those of Auguste Perret and his imitators – are classical in this way: that is to say, they are thought out in modern materials but in a classical spirit and sealed as classical only by the tiniest allusive gestures. In the last section of the book I shall have more to say about all this. In the meantime the thing which it is quite essential for us to understand before we go any further is this question of the orders – the 'five orders of architecture'. Everybody has heard of them, but what exactly are they? Why are there five and not four, or sixteen or three hundred and twenty-six?

*117*

One thing at a time. First, what are the orders? On page 126 you will find a very clear diagram of the Doric order. It consists, you see, of a temple column standing on a pedestal and carrying on its head the architrave, frieze and cornice, those elements which are collectively called the entablature. Then, in plates 1–4 you see the Doric order again, with its four companions; it is the second from the left, with the Tuscan to the left, the Ionic, Corinthian and Composite to the right.

9

An 'order' is the 'column-and-superstructure' unit of a temple colonnade. It does not *have* to have a pedestal and often does not. It *does* have to have an entablature (columns are meaningless unless they support something), and the cornice represents the eaves.

Now, why are there five orders? This is a little more difficult and it is necessary to glance back to some origins. The earliest written description of any of the orders is in Vitruvius. The name of this Roman author will crop up frequently in this book and this is the moment to introduce him. He was an architect of some consequence in the reign of Augustus and wrote a treatise in ten books, *De Architectura*, which he dedicated to the Emperor. This is the only treatise of its kind to have survived from antiquity and for that reason has been accorded enormous veneration. Vitruvius was not himself a man of any great genius or literary talent or indeed – for all we know – of architectural talent. The thing about his treatise is that it rounds up and preserves for us an immense quantity of traditional building lore: it is the code of practice of a Roman architect of the first century AD, enriched with instances and historical notes.

In the course of Vitruvius's third and fourth books he describes three of the orders – Ionic, Doric and Corinthian – and gives a few notes on another, the Tuscan. He tells us in which part of the world each was invented. He relates them to his descriptions of temples and tells us to which gods and goddesses each order is appropriate. His descriptions are by no means exhaustive, he gives no fifth order, he does not present them in what we think of as the 'proper' sequence (Tuscan, Doric, Ionic, Corinthian) and – most important – he does not present them as a set of canonical formulae embodying all architectural virtue. That was left for the theorists of the Renaissance.

In the middle of the fifteenth century, fourteen hundred years after Vitruvius, the Florentine architect and humanist, Leon Battista Alberti, described the orders, partly with reference to Vitruvius and partly from his own observations of Roman remains. It was he who added, from observation, a fifth order – the Composite – which combines features of the Corinthian with those of the Ionic. But Alberti was still perfectly objective and Vitruvian in his attitude. It was Sebastiano Serlio, nearly a century later, who really started the orders – the five orders now – on their long career of canonical, symbolic, almost legendary, authority. I am not sure that Serlio quite meant to do this but that is what he did.

Serlio was a man of the High Renaissance, an exact contemporary of Michelangelo, a near contemporary of Raphael and an associate of the architect-painter Baldassare Peruzzi whose designs he inherited. He built a few quite important buildings but his greatest service to architecture was to compile the first full-scale fully illustrated architectural grammar of the Renaissance. It came out as a series of books. The first two appeared in Venice, the later books in France under the patronage of François I. The books became the architectural bible of the civilized world. The Italians used them, the French owed nearly everything to Serlio and his books, the Germans and Flemings based their own books on his, the Elizabethans cribbed from him and Sir Christopher Wren was still finding Serlio invaluable when he built the Sheldonian at Oxford in 1663.

Serlio's book on the orders starts with an engraving – the very first *1* of its kind – in which all five orders are shown standing side by side like ill-assorted ninepins ranged according to their relative slimness, that is to say, according to the ratio of lower diameter to height. All are on pedestals. The stubby Tuscan is on the left; then the similar but slightly taller Doric; the elegant Ionic; the lofty, elaborate Corinthian; and finally the still more elongated and further enriched Composite. In the text accompanying this plate Serlio explains himself. He says that just as the ancient dramatists used to preface their plays with a prologue telling audiences what it was all going to be about, so he is putting before us the principal characters in his treatise on architecture. He does it in a way which makes the orders seem as categorical in the grammar of architecture as, say, the four conjugations of verbs in the grammar of the Latin language.

This very effective and, quite literally, dramatic gesture of Serlio's was not lost upon his successors, and the five orders as a 'complete set', all deviations from which were questionable, passed from hand to hand. Nearly all seventeenth- and eighteenth-century primers of architecture start in the same way, with a plate of the five columns and entablatures ranged side by side – Bloem in Switzerland, De Vries in Flanders, Dietterlin in Germany, Fréart and Perrault in France and, in England, Shute, Gibbs and Sir William Chambers. George Gwilt's edition of Chambers carries us up to 1825 and if you go from this to the same author's *Encyclopedia of Architecture* and follow this work to its latest edition in 1891 you will find it still being stated there that 'in the proper understanding and application of the orders is laid the foundation of architecture as an art'. When I was a student in the Bartlett School at University College, London, it was taken for granted that one's first task as a student was to draw out in great detail three of the classical orders.

Now there are two important points about all this. The first is to realize that although the Romans clearly accepted the individuality of Doric, Ionic and Corinthian, and knew about their historical origins, it was not they who embalmed and sanctified them in the arbitrary, limiting way with which we are familiar. The second point is to realize the immense importance, for the whole of architecture since the Renaissance, of this process of embalming, of canonization. The orders came to be regarded as the very touchstone of architecture, as architectural instruments of the greatest possible subtlety, embodying all the ancient wisdom of mankind in the building art – almost, in fact, as products of nature herself. And this is where the modern eye must often confess itself defeated. Unless you really *know* your orders and can recognize, at a glance, a Tuscan according to Vitruvius, a Corinthian from the Temple of Vespasian or an Ionic from the Temple of Saturn or the rather odd Composite concocted by Serlio from the Colosseum you will not appreciate all the refinements and variations which, from time to time, have been lovingly and assiduously applied to them. Nevertheless, even an 'O level' understanding of the orders is something, for it is by no means only in the handling of the orders themselves that the character of classical architecture lies. It is also – even more (much more, in fact) – in the way they are deployed; but that is a subject for another chapter.

Meanwhile, let us be quite clear about how variable or how invariable the orders are. Serlio puts them before us with a tremendous air of authority giving dimensions for each part as if to settle the profiles and proportions once and for all. But in fact, Serlio's orders, while obviously reflecting Vitruvius to some extent, are also based on his own observation of ancient monuments and thus, by a process of personal selection, to quite a considerable degree are his own invention. It could hardly be otherwise. Vitruvius's descriptions have gaps in them and these can only be filled from knowledge of surviving Roman monuments themselves. The orders as exemplified in these monuments vary considerably from one to the other so it is open to anybody to abstract what he considers the best features of each in order to set out what he considers his ideal Corinthian, Ionic or whatever it is. All through the history of classical architecture speculation as to the ideal types of each of the orders has continued, oscillating between antiquarian reverence on the one hand and sheer personal invention on the other. Somewhere between the extremes have been the types composed and published by the great theorists: Serlio, of course, first in 1537, then Vignola in 1562, Palladio in 1570 and Scamozzi in 1615. These have had a normalizing effect all over the world. But in all the centuries there have been instances where architects have taken pride in copying specific antique examples. For instance, Jean Bullant at Écouen, the great house near Paris, derived the Corinthian with most of its ornaments from the Temple of Castor and Pollux; that was in 1540. Inigo Jones at Covent Garden in 1630 reconstructed the Tuscan on the basis of Vitruvius's text – almost an archaeological exercise. Then Sir John Soane in 1793 borrowed literally from the Temple of Vesta at Tivoli for the Bank of England. On the other hand, there have always been daring innovators. Philibert de l'Orme invented a new 'French' order for the Tuileries Palace; Wendel Dietterlin's orders in his book of 1594 are phantasmagoric variations on Serlio; Borromini's orders are outrageous and extremely expressive inventions, entirely his own So it is a mistake ever to think of the five orders of architecture as a sort of child's box of bricks which architects have used to save themselves the trouble of inventing. It is much better to think of them as grammatical expressions imposing a formidable discipline, but a discipline within which personal sensibility always has a certain play – a discipline, moreover, which can sometimes be burst asunder by a flight of poetic genius.

Now, at this point I am going to ask you to look again at the Doric order. Because I think it may still puzzle you that the entablature has so many curious bits and pieces, all with names but with no particular decorative or symbolic value that you can see. Why mutules? Why triglyphs and metopes? Why the taenia and those odd little tassels called guttae? You may well ask. And I can only give you a very general answer. It is quite certain that the Doric order derives its forms from a primitive type of timber construction. Vitruvius tells us as much. When you are looking at a Doric order executed in stone you are looking, in effect, at a carved representation of a Doric order constructed of wood. Not a literal representation, of course, but a sculptural equivalent. The earliest temples in the ancient world were of wood. Gradually some of these temples – those, doubtless, of special sanctity and which attracted wealth – came to be rebuilt in stone. It would be felt imperative to preserve in the more permanent stone version the actual forms round which so much sanctity had gathered. Hence, the carpentry devices of the wooden entablature, already, no doubt, somewhat stylized, were copied in stone or marble. Later on, no doubt, stone temples on new sites copied the copies, and so it went on till the whole thing became a static and accepted formula.

Look at the Doric entablature again in the light of this and it does, to some extent, explain itself. The *mutules* seem to be the ends of cantilevers jutting out to support the eaves and to carry the eaves, from which the rain drips, well away from the columns. Then the *triglyphs* could be the ends of cross beams resting on the architrave. The *taenia* looks like some kind of binding member and it appears to be secured to the triglyphs by the *guttae*, which are not tassels, of course, but pegs. I say 'seem to be', 'could be', 'looks like' because all these things are my own rough guesses. Some archaeologists have devoted much ingenuity to trying to work back from the formalized Doric to its last timber prototype. Their guesses are worth more than mine, but guesses they are and are likely to remain. All that matters for us now is that in the process of time a system of timber construction, copied in stone, crystallized into the linguistic formula which Vitruvius knew, and so we know, as the Doric order. This crystallization has a very obvious parallel in language. Words, expressions, grammatical constructions have all at some time had to be invented to meet particular needs of communication. Those immediate needs are long since forgotten, but the words and their patterns still form the language we use for a thousand purposes – including poetry. That is how it is with the five orders of architecture.

One more word about the orders. They are always supposed to have something resembling personalities; Vitruvius was perhaps responsible for this. The Doric he saw as exemplifying 'the proportion, strength and grace of a man's body' – presumably an average well-built male. The Ionic, for him, was characterized by 'feminine slenderness' and the Corinthian as imitating 'the slight figure of a girl', which may seem not very different from the last. But Vitruvius having opened the door to personalization of the orders the Renaissance let in a lot more – often very contradictory. Thus while Scamozzi echoes Vitruvius in calling the Corinthian 'virginal', Sir

Henry Wotton, a few years later, distorts him by calling it 'lascivious' and 'decked like a wanton courtezan', adding that the morals of Corinth were bad anyway. Nevertheless, the Corinthian has always been regarded as female and the Doric as male, with the Ionic in between as something rather unsexed – an ageing scholar or a calm and gentle matron. Serlio's recommendations are perhaps the most specific and consistent. The Doric, he says, should be used for churches dedicated to the more extroverted male saints (St Paul, St Peter or St George) and to militant types in general; the Ionic for matronly saints, neither too tough nor too tender, and also for men of learning; the Corinthian for virgins, most especially the Virgin Mary. To the Composite Serlio awards no special characteristics, while the Tuscan he finds suitable for fortifications and prisons.

Now there is no need to take any of this too seriously. Certainly, there is no need when you are looking at the Corinthian columns of, say, the Mansion House in London, to wonder if the Lord Mayor who commissioned them thought of them as virginal or the other thing. The fact is that the orders have mostly been used according to taste, according to circumstances and very often according to means; building in plain Tuscan or Doric was obviously less expensive than building in richly carved Corinthian. There *are* cases where the use of an order has a deliberate symbolic significance. I think, for instance, that Wren must have used Doric at Chelsea Hospital because of its soldierly character. And there is the fascinating case of Inigo Jones and the Tuscan at Covent Garden. Tuscan and Doric are the two most primitive orders and architects have tended to use them when they wanted to express roughness and toughness or in the case of the Doric what is called a 'soldierly bearing'. At the other end of the scale the Composite is sometimes chosen because the architect wants to lay it on thick – luxury, opulence, no expense spared.

Anyway, the main point is this. The orders provided a sort of *gamut* of architectural character all the way from the rough and tough to the slim and fine. In true classical designing the selection of the order is a very vital point – it is a choice of mood. What you do with the order, what exact ratios you give its different parts, what enrichments you put in or leave out, this again shifts and defines the mood.

Well, so much for the five orders of architecture – five basic elements in the architectural grammar of antiquity. But what can you do with the orders? How does the grammar work?

TOSCANO DORICO IONICO CORINTHO COMPOSITO

2

## The progress of the five orders

Each generation succeeding Serlio's studied the orders afresh and delineated them with carefully argued variations. **2** Vignola's versions, the first to be engraved on copper, appeared in 1563. Palladio's exposition followed in 1570 but gave no plate showing the five orders together. **3** Scamozzi's wood-engraving of 1615, however, is much in the spirit of Palladio. **4** Claude Perrault, the Frenchman, consulted all the Italian authorities and produced his own copper-plate versions in 1676, with a modular scale from which the proportions of the various parts could be read and memorized.

3

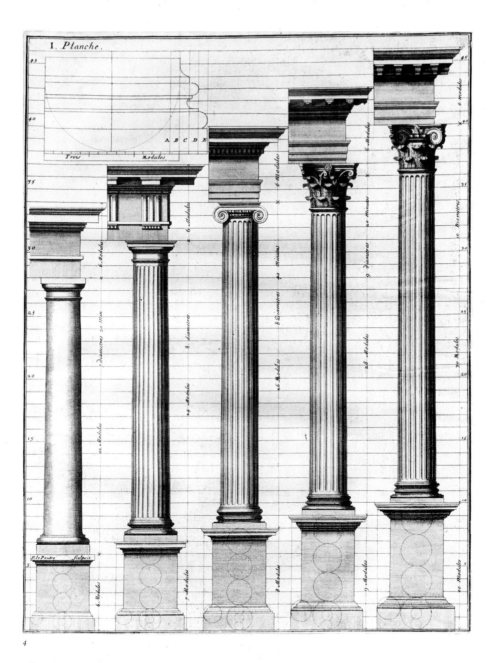

I. Planche.

A B C D E

Trou     Modules

F. le Pautre    sculpsit

4

6

7

5

**5** Philibert de l'Orme's 'French order' (1567) gave logical expression to the fact that a column was composed of several separate stones. **6** A Corinthian capital by Borromini with inverted foliations. **7** Ionic on a square plan; from Fréart, 1650.

# CHAPTER TWO

## The Grammar of Antiquity

So far, I have concentrated on the five orders. From now on, however, I shall take your familiarity with them for granted and talk less about the orders themselves than about how they are used. Just look for the last time at plate 1. These orders, what are they? They are columns supported on pedestals (whose use is optional) and carrying beams with projections to support the eaves of a roof. What can you do with them? Well, if you are designing a temple with porticos at front and back and colonnades at the sides, these columns and their appurtenances account for very nearly everything, so far as the exterior is concerned. At each of the four corners of the temple, the gable splits off from the cornice to form, front and back, that flat triangular shape which is called a pediment; and there you are. But suppose you are *not* designing a temple. Suppose you are designing a large and complicated structure like a theatre or courts of justice, a structure of several storeys involving arches and vaults and many windows and doors, what then? Common sense would suggest that you then scrap the orders as being irrevocably associated with temples and start all over again, letting your arches and vaults and window-patterns find an expression of their own. That may be modern common sense but it is not what happened and it is not the view the Romans took when they adopted the arch and the vault for their public buildings. Far from leaving the orders out when they built vaulted amphitheatres, basilicas and triumphal arches, they brought them in, in the most conspicuous way possible, as if they felt (which perhaps they did) that no building could communicate anything unless the orders were involved in it. To them, the orders *were* architecture. Perhaps it was, in the first instance, a question of carrying over the prestige of temple architecture into great secular projects. I do not know. Anyway, the Romans took this highly stylized but structurally quite primitive kind of architecture and married it to arched and vaulted multi-storey buildings of great elaboration. And in doing so they raised architectural language to a new level. They invented ways of using the orders not merely as ornamental enrichments for their new types of structure but as controls. The orders are, in many Roman buildings, quite useless structurally but they make their buildings expressive, they make them speak; they conduct the building, with sense and ceremony and often with great elegance, into the mind of the beholder. Visually, they dominate and control the buildings to which they are attached.

How is this done? Not just by pinning columns and entablatures and pediments on to an otherwise bare structure. The whole thing – structure and architectural expression – must be integrated, and this means that columns must be introduced in a variety of different ways. You see, there are columns and columns. Columns in the round have to carry something. Mostly they carry their own entablature and perhaps a wall or perhaps only the eaves of a roof above it. But you can have what are called 'detached columns' which have a wall behind them which they just do not touch but into which their entablature is firmly built. Then you can have three-quarter columns, one quarter of each being buried in the wall. Similarly you can have half columns, half buried in the wall. And finally you can have 'pilasters' which are flat representations of columns, carved as it were in relief on the wall (or you can think of them, if you like, as built-in square columns). There you have four degrees of integration of an order in a structure – four degrees of relief, four strengths of shadow. The Romans never learnt to exploit the full possibilities of this, though they showed the way. To illustrate most forcibly what I have been saying I suggest you look at plates 72, 73, 74 and 75: four church façades of the sixteenth–seventeenth centuries. The Gesù, Rome, is mostly pilasters. S. Susanna has pilasters above and pilasters, half columns and three-quarter columns below. The Val de Grâce in Paris has a porch with columns in the round, half columns, three-quarter columns and pilasters. I shall have more to say about these three buildings later on. Just now, I am trying to get your eye in to the kinds of play which become possible with the orders as a very long-term result of what the Romans pioneered. And while you are looking at these four churches note one other thing. Every time an order changes its plane of relief, say from pilaster forward to half, from half forward again to three-quarter, the entablature has to break forward too. You cannot dodge columns about under an unchanging entablature. That is one of the rules.

You will understand from all this, I think, just what I mean when I say that in the classical language the orders are not merely pinned on to the structure but integrated with it. Sometimes they sink right into it, sometimes they come walking out of it into a free-standing porch or colonnade. And all the time they *control* it.

Now back to ancient Rome. I emphasized earlier that all major Roman buildings other than temples were designed on the basis of arches and vaults, whereas the orders belong strictly to the more primitive system of 'trabeation' – that is to say, post and lintel construction. To marry the two in the sense of giving the old types of temple column the job of carrying arches could work up to a point but it was never satisfactory for two reasons. First, because the columns and their entablatures had become so closely identified by long association as one thing, that to divorce them meant a sort of mutilation. Second, because arched and vaulted buildings of any size require not columns but massive piers to take the loads. Columns are too slender. So what did the Romans do? The Colosseum at Rome answers the question at once. Plate 12 shows the least damaged side of that astonishing building. Here you see its three interminable open galleries – arch upon arch, with an additional solid storey at the top. And you see that every row of arches is framed inside a continuous colonnade. The colonnades have no structural purpose – or very little. They are representations of temple architecture carved, as it were, in relief on a building which is not a temple, which is multi-storeyed and is built as a system of arches and vaults.

If this way of combining the arcuated and trabeated systems – treating the trabeated system simply as a means of expression – seems to us absurdly simple, that is chiefly because we are so used to it. It *is* simple, but when you begin to examine it in detail, not as simple as all that. We have here in the Colosseum four orders: Doric on the ground floor, Ionic on the next, Corinthian on the uppermost open storey and on the plain storey above an indeterminate order (which has sometimes been called Composite but which is in fact unique to the Colosseum). Now focus on one bay of one of the open storeys – say of the middle storey which is Ionic. Plate 16 is a measured drawing of one such bay. Here you have a grammatical construction which is a pretty complete thing. It is controlled by an Ionic order which obeys nothing but its own traditional aesthetic rules. The shape and size of the piers behind the columns and of the arch, on the other hand, have come about through the exigencies of convenience and construction. The two disciplines have got to meet each other harmoniously and I think we may agree that they do. The pedestal moulding of the order ranges with the sill height of the arched gallery. The impost of the arch strikes the columns a little above half their height and the arch sits comfortably between the columns and the architrave above. If this arrangement is satisfactory it has been achieved by a very careful balancing of needs, the aesthetic dictatorship of the Ionic order and the practical needs of the building as a thing of use. A quite slight alteration to any part would wreck the whole thing. If for instance, you widened the opening by twelve inches, what would happen? The crown of the arch would go up by six inches. Assuming you want to keep the existing space between arch and entablature, the entablature would go up by six inches; so the columns would become six inches taller; and the rules of the Ionic order being what they are every other part of the order would have to be bigger. The pedestal would grow so its moulding would no longer range with the sill height and, worse still, the entablature, which you have already raised by six inches, would now grow in height and probably make trouble with the floor levels above, to say nothing of the upstairs order, the Corinthian.

To be frank, I think this bay of the Colosseum is capable of a little more 'tolerance' than I have represented. But you will begin to see the kind of discipline which is involved in the classical language and which is inherent in it. And this discipline can be tightened. Look now at plate 17. Here is the same arrangement, in principle, in a theoretical design by the sixteenth-century architect, Vignola. Vignola has obviously been determined to produce something in which all the parts are absolutely dependent on all the others. There is no tolerance whatever round the arch. The piers are only just wide enough to receive the archivolt and the returns of the pedestal mouldings. The thing is as tight as a knot. If this design, as interpreted on your drawing-board, to your chosen scale, does not come naturally to terms with your planning and structural needs – well, you have got to play the game another way. And, of course, there are other ways, plenty, if you can think of them.

The Colosseum, which started us on this theme of arch and order in combination, was, as you can imagine, one of the buildings from which the men of the Renaissance learnt most. It exemplifies not only this particular combination but also the superimposition of orders and, in the top storey, the use of a pilaster order to render expressive a plain, almost windowless wall. There were other buildings of this class, the Theatre of Marcellus, for instance; and, outside Rome, the theatres at Verona and at Pola in Istria. All were closely studied, and useful grammatical elements extracted from them; they were published by Serlio and a generation later by Palladio. If you want to see Colosseum themes reflected in the works of Renaissance masters, here are three instances, more or less at random, among the illustrations: the Palazzo Corner, Venice, with its superimposed *36* columns and arches; the Ducal Palace at Mantua, where Giulio *49* Romano romanticizes the same theme; or, for the pilastered upper storey of the Colosseum, the Castello Farnese at Caprarola. Very *60* different buildings indeed, but using those grammatical expressions of which the Colosseum was the most conspicuous exemplar.

Perhaps even more instructive, grammatically, than the theatres were the triumphal arches of Rome and other parts of Italy; Serlio gives as many as eleven. These arches, being purely ceremonial affairs, made great play with architectural and sculptural detail. In Rome, the largest and most important were and still are the Arch of Septimius Severus and the Arch of Constantine. Now, look at the latter. What *19* does it consist of? It is a massive rectangular slab of masonry with three holes in it – the centre hole is the main arch, the other two are lower and narrower subsidiary arches. Set against the four piers dividing the arches are four columns, standing on pedestals and rising to an entablature, which breaks out over each separate column and at each of those points of breaking out carries a carved standing figure. Above the entablature is a superstructure called an 'attic' storey. It makes a background for the figures and is carved in relief and lettered.

Now, observe the arrangement of all these elements. The keystone of the centre arch is hard up against the bottom of the entablature. The keystones of the side arches are hard up against a line which is that of the impost of the centre arch; and the three arches are all of the same ratio of height to width. The depth of the entablature is exactly such that the appropriate column, with its pedestal, fills the space between entablature and ground: an interesting, compact and harmonious arrangement admirably fulfilling its symbolic function. In the fifteenth century this arch and the other Roman arches had an enormous imaginative appeal both for painters and for architects (who, of course, often were painters) and, as a consequence, we find, over and over again, features and combinations of features, which originated in the triumphal arches, being used in totally different sorts of buildings, all sorts of buildings, and used, once again, as grammatical expressions controlling the structure.

By far the most impressive case of this is the conversion of the triumphal arch into a Christian church. This was achieved by Leon Battista Alberti. At Rimini, when he designed what we know as the Tempio Malatestiano, Alberti gave it a west front manifestly based on the Roman triumphal arch just outside the town. But that was only the first step. Much later, towards the end of his life, he designed the church of S. Andrea at Mantua and here he not only adapted the triumphal arch idea to the west front but brought it inside and made it the model for his nave arcades; and, more than that, he designed the west front and the arcades to the same scale, so that the whole church, inside and out, is, as it were, a logical three-dimensional extension of the triumphal arch idea. I have deliberately kept the exterior small because I much doubt Alberti's responsibility for some of its features – he died before it was built. But the main idea is clear enough and you will see how it is echoed again in the interior, though here I must warn you against the frippery eighteenth-century wall decoration which in photographs always robs this building of much of its force. Here was a real triumph – at the same time a conquest of Roman grammar and the creation of a continuously logical structure on the model of which I do not know how many classical churches were to be built in the next four centuries. S. Andrea, Mantua, is the first great step towards St Peter's, Rome, and St Paul's, London.

There is much more I could say about triumphal arches and their contribution to the classical language. The most elementary fact of all about them – the division of a space by columns into three unequal parts: narrow, wide, narrow – is perhaps also the most important. Plate 50 is a design for a gateway by Giulio Romano, obviously on the triumphal arch model. But the triumphal arch rhythm – narrow, wide, narrow – is also implicit in other buildings by the same artist. At a much later date, the attic storey was often found to be a useful element and a good background for figures. There is one at Somerset House, though frankly I do not think it much helps the design in that instance. A really fine handling of an attic storey with figures is C.R. Cockerell's Ashmolean building at Oxford.

24

So now we have glanced at two types of Roman building – the galleried amphitheatre type, instanced by the Colosseum, and the triumphal arch type – and seen the extent to which they were exploited as sources of grammatical expression. There are many other types of Roman architecture but none, I think, which was so completely digested and became so much an organic part of the classical language as these. There were the baths, of course, whose *24, 25* grandiose planning and vaulted halls and chambers became leading inspirations on certain occasions. There was the unique Pantheon, the *27* prototype of all great classical domes; and the vast Basilica of Constantine, the challenge to all builders of great vaulted naves. And, of course, there were the temples. It is a curious fact that the typical Roman temple – the rectangular building with an open portico and *8* pediment in front and with or without columns or pilasters all round (in fact, what we think of as the most obvious symbol of Roman architecture) – was never used as a model for churches in Italy and never, indeed, in Europe till the eighteenth century. The circular *31* temple, on the other hand, did play an important part. This was chiefly, perhaps, because of its very beautiful re-creation by *32* Bramante, which I shall be describing later on.

But the great achievement of the Renaissance was not the strict imitation of Roman buildings (that was left for the eighteenth and nineteenth centuries) but the re-establishment of the grammar of antiquity as a universal discipline – *the* discipline, inherited from the remote past of mankind and applicable to all honourable building enterprises whatever. Of that grammar, that discipline, I have already perhaps said enough to convince you of its reality and also of its simplicity, but there is a little more you should know. There is, for instance, the very simple matter indeed of the spacing of columns – what is technically called 'intercolumniation'. Intercolumniation sets the 'tempo' of a building and once the tempo is set you cannot play fast and loose with it. Variations within the tempo, yes, but of specific and significant kinds.

The Romans attached so much importance to the spacing of columns that they established five standard types, measured in column diameters. Vitruvius records them. The closest spacing they called *Pycnostyle* – $1\frac{1}{2}$ diameters. Then came *Systyle, Eustyle, Diastyle* and finally the widest, *Araeostyle*, at 4 diameters. *Systyle* and *Eustyle* are the commonest. *Systyle* you might describe as a quick march,

*Eustyle* as an easy dignified walk. The extreme intercolumniations neither march nor walk. *Pycnostyle* always seems to me to mean 'halt' – a palisade of men drawn up to attention. *Araeostyle* is a very long stride indeed, almost a slow leaping motion. If you like you can try to equate the intercolumniation with musical terminology. I would suggest, for *Diastyle*, 'adagio', for *Eustyle*, 'andante' and for *Systyle*, 'allegro'; but I do not like 'presto' for *Pycnostyle*, still less 'largo' for *Araeostyle*. As with all analogies of this sort it is nonsense to press it too far. But the importance of intercolumniation – this system of 'beating time' in architecture – is, of course, immense. In plates 32 and 34 there is a telling contrast which puts the whole thing in a nutshell. Here are buildings of the same general shape and roughly the same commemorative purpose. But how different the emotions they arouse: Bramante's *Diastyle* (3 diameters), stately, serene, meditative; Hawksmoor's *Pycnostyle* ($1\frac{1}{2}$ diameters), tense and forbidding, a ceremonial palisade. And if you look through the other illustrations with this question of 'tempo' in mind you will be in no doubt about the importance of intercolumniation. You will also begin to see the kind of variations which can be introduced – coupled columns, spaced pairs of columns, columns in the narrow, wide, narrow rhythm of the triumphal arch and the really intricate rhythms you get when columns, half columns and three-quarter columns begin to play together, sometimes (as in the church façades we looked at earlier on) leaving the basic tempo a matter of some doubt.

I have been talking all this time about grammar and about rules, to the extent that you may have begun to see the classical language as a frighteningly impersonal and intractable thing, something which challenges the architect at every turn, knocks his intuitions for six and allows him only a tiny margin of freedom in the choice of this rather than that. If you have received that impression I am not altogether sorry because that *is* part of the game. But there is something else: the architect's identification of himself with the very elements which defy him, so that he is intensely *with* the orders he is using as well as *up against* them, so that he almost believes himself to have designed the order whose manipulation gives him so many headaches. I cannot possibly illustrate this better than by quoting some remarks by a very great classical architect of a previous generation, Sir Edwin Lutyens. Lutyens was brought up in the picturesque 'Old English' tradition of the late nineteenth century and to that tradition all his early houses belong. When he was thirty-five, however, in 1903, he began to have precisely those insights into the nature of classicism which were to make him eventually one of the architectural masters of his time. He was designing a house for a rich manufacturer at Ilkley when the splendour of the classical discipline seized him, and in a letter to his friend Herbert Baker he put down some wonderfully vivid flashes of thought:

> That time-worn doric order – a lovely thing – I have the cheek to adopt. You can't copy it. To be right you have to take it and design it. . . . You cannot copy: you find if you do you are caught, a mess remains.
>
> It means hard labour, hard thinking, over every line in all three dimensions and in every joint; and no stone can be allowed to slide. If you tackle it in this way, the Order belongs to you, and every stroke, being mentally handled, must become endowed with such poetry and artistry as God has given you. You alter one feature (which you have to, always), then every other feature has to sympathise and undergo some care and invention. Therefore it is no mean game, nor is it a game you can play lightheartedly.

'You can't copy', says Lutyens. But on the other hand, in another letter:

> You cannot play originality with the Orders. They have to be so well digested that there is nothing but essence left. When right they are curiously lovely – unalterable as plant forms. . . . The perfection of the Order is far nearer nature than anything produced on impulse or accident-wise.

There was an architect who really knew, because he learnt for himself, what the classical language meant. He loved, obeyed and defied the orders all at the same time. If the understanding of rule is one basic factor in the creation of great classical buildings the defiance of rule is the other.

8

## The temple

The orders developed as temple architecture, but the temple form itself was never copied till the eighteenth and nineteenth centuries. It was the eloquence of the column with the moulded profiles above it that seized the imagination of the Renaissance. Only when classical antiquity began to be seen in a much wider historical perspective was the temple form revived and then more often as a secular power-symbol than as a religious building. **8** The best preserved of all Roman temples is the Corinthian Maison Carrée at Nîmes (*c.* AD 130). **9** In Paris, the Madeleine, begun as a church, was continued by Napoleon as a Temple of Glory but was completed as a church in 1842. **10** Sixteen and a half centuries after the Maison Carrée Thomas Jefferson began to build the Capitol of the State of Virginia (Richmond, USA) as an Ionic temple. **11** At Birmingham, a competition for a new town hall was won in 1832 by Joseph Hansom with a design which competes valiantly with the antique.

28

9

10

11

12

## Order upon order

The Romans took the orders from temple architecture and manipulated them to decorate and control their secular monuments. When these rose to several storeys, each storey was given its appropriate order – the strong, plain Doric below, then the lighter Ionic, followed by the elegant Corinthian and perhaps at the top a Composite. **12** The Colosseum, Rome (1st century AD) is the most spectacular ancient example of orders superimposed.

13

**13** Alberti, in the mid-fifteenth century, reintroduced the idea of superimposition in the Palazzo Rucellai, Florence.
**14** At Oxford, the Jacobean masons who designed the Schools in 1613 displayed their learning by mounting all five orders on a Tudor-style gateway.
**15** St Gervais, Paris, by Salomon de Brosse, 1616–21, introduces three superimposed orders in a highly sophisticated design.

14

15

16

## The order and the arch

The orders are fundamentally a trabeated (post and beam) system. How to combine this with an arcuated system was a Roman problem. Framed within a pair of columns and an entablature, an arch must have a decisive relationship at its springing and its crown. **16** Elevation of one bay at the second (Ionic) stage of the Colosseum. **17** The same theme as interpreted by Vignola, 1563. In this tightly knit version no single dimension can be changed without affecting the proportions of the order and thus of the whole design. **18** Bramante's pioneering essay on this theme in the cloister of S. Maria della Pace, Rome, 1500–04.

17

19

## The triumphal arch

The Roman triumphal arch, as a type, was one of the main sources of Renaissance expression with its tripartite division of four equal columns unequally spaced. **19** The Arch of Constantine, the largest to survive, supplied the idea of the 'detached' column with returning entablature and the superincumbent 'attic storey'. **20** Alberti's early façade of the Tempio Malatestiano, Rimini, is manifestly based on the triumphal arch scheme.

20

21

21 At S. Andrea, Mantua (1472), he applied it to
the west front but replaced the attic storey by a
pediment. 22 In the interior of the same church
the arches and the pilastered piers read like a
succession of triumphal arches. 23 The intense
fascination of Roman architecture in the
Renaissance world is also reflected in painting:
detail from Mantegna's *Martyrdom of St Sebastian*
in the Louvre.

23

22

25

## Roman baths

The remains of the Roman baths (*thermae*) constituted a vast heritage of architectural material. Their complex plans suggested spatial arrangements of various kinds and their vaulted halls became prototypes of public buildings of the railway age. **24** The *tepidarium* of the Baths of Diocletian, Rome, converted by Michelangelo (1563) into the church of S. Maria degli Angeli. **25** Plan of the Baths of Titus, as restored by Palladio whose drawings were collected by Lord Burlington and published in 1730. **26** The concourse of Pennsylvania Railroad Station, New York (1906–10, demolished 1965), designed by McKim, Mead and White in imitation of the central hall of the Baths of Caracalla.

26

Veduta del Pantheon d'Agrippa
oggi Chiesa di S. Maria ad Martires

27

28

DEIPARAE IN COELVM ASSVMPTAE

## The Pantheon theme

The Pantheon is a Roman temple of unique form, due to the special circumstances of its construction over a long period. The combination of a domed cylindrical body and projecting portico finds echoes in the seventeenth century and later.

**27** Piranesi's etching of the Pantheon as it was in 1760. **28** Bernini's interpretation of the theme at S. Maria dell'Assunta, Ariccia, near Rome (1664). **29** A miniature domestic Pantheon on an island in Lake Windermere – 'Belle Isle', designed by John Plaw, 1774–75. **30** The library building which dominates the University of Virginia, Charlottesville, designed by Thomas Jefferson and built in 1817–26.

# CHAPTER THREE

## Sixteenth-Century Linguistics

I have been concerned with the grammatical workings of classical architecture – the mechanics of it: the nature of the five orders; columns, three-quarter and half columns; pilasters; the conjunction of columns with arches; intercolumniation, and all that. Now, getting a little warmer, I am going to talk about the handling of this grammar by some of the great innovating personalities of the sixteenth century and first of all by Donato Bramante.

The reason I go straight for Bramante is this. It was he, more than anybody else, who re-established the grammar of ancient Rome in buildings of pre-eminent consequence. I am not forgetting the performances of some of his predecessors: of Alberti, who, as we saw earlier, generated the perfect model for a classical church out of the Roman triumphal arch; of Brunelleschi, who, earlier still, gave new breath to the Corinthian order in the naves of his Florentine churches. But it was Bramante who set the seal on all this, who stated firmly and finally: 'this is the Roman language – this and no other is the way to use it'. Everybody recognized his authority. Serlio wrote that he was the man who revived the buried architecture of antiquity; and Serlio paid Bramante an even greater tribute when he included some of his works in the part of his book ostensibly devoted entirely to ancient Rome. For Serlio, Bramante was the exact equivalent of the antique.

Before Bramante came to Rome in 1499 he had worked in Milan in the court circle in which Leonardo da Vinci was the phenomenal presence. Leonardo was interested philosophically, diagrammatically, in architecture rather than in working it out in the orthodox forms of the antique. Bramante was interested in both, but more precisely in the working out, and you can still see in Milan, tucked crookedly away off one of the busiest streets, his earliest work, the strange little church of S. Maria presso S. Satiro, with its nave of piers, pilasters and arches and its choir which is not there at all but is only represented in a marvellous perspective representation in low relief.

When Bramante came to Rome and entered the service of the

Pope, he was already fifty-five and had only another sixteen years to live. But they were tremendously full years. Among other things he designed and partly built the new St Peter's and two great courts in the Vatican and if this book were supposed to be a history of classical architecture I would have to settle down at this point to describing them. But I am quite content, for my present purpose, to take one building by Bramante and ask you to look at it rather closely. It is illustrated in plate 32: the Tempietto (little temple) in the cloister of S. Pietro in Montorio, Rome, built in 1502 on the traditional site of St Peter's martyrdom. This building is a reconstruction by Bramante of an ancient Roman circular temple – or so it seems at first. Preceding it I illustrate a real antique, the so-called Temple of Vesta on the bank of *31* the Tiber; it has lost the whole of its entablature and the rather pretty pantiled hat it wears is just a makeshift. But there (or in a temple of that sort) is Bramante's theme. He transposes it from Corinthian to Doric (Doric, perhaps, as appropriate to St Peter's militant sainthood). He mounts it on three steps and sets a continuous moulded plinth under the order. This plinth (which Serlio carelessly omitted in his engraving) gives the little building a sudden and auspicious 'lift', enough to ratify its sanctity. Then comes the Doric order, then the balustrade. And each Doric column has an answering Doric pilaster on the wall of the inner building – what is called the *cella*. This cella rises higher than the colonnade and is covered with a hemispherical dome (or rather, was covered; the dome was later slightly altered). Now, is this a literal reconstruction of a Roman temple or is it not? Clearly not. It is an *extension* of an idea borrowed from the Romans. The plinth and the vertical penetration of the central cylinder up and through to a hemispherical dome are Bramante's inventions and highly successful ones to judge by the number of times they have been imitated.

This Tempietto is a perfect piece of architectural prose – a statement, clear as a bell. Through Serlio's regrettably inaccurate engraving and, later, Palladio's more accurate one, the building became world-famous, as famous almost as the Pantheon or the Arch of Constantine and as much a 'classic'. Sir Christopher Wren knew it of course, through Palladio, and at one phase in the designing of St Paul's he tried using two Bramante temples as the top stages of his two western towers. That was while he was still struggling with all sorts of unmanageable alternatives for the great drum and dome over the

Cathedral's transeptal space. Eventually it dawned on him that the Tempietto was the clue to that problem even more than to the other, in spite of the enormous difference in size and site. Look at St Paul's

33    dome and you will see at once just how much it owes to the Tempietto. But the more you look the more you will see that St Paul's dome is no mere enlargement of the Tempietto. The Tempietto has 16 columns: Wren required twice as many. A ring of 32 columns, Wren saw, would lack stable orientation; so he filled up every fourth intercolumniation – those which come over the great piers – and carved a niche in each, thus giving his colonnade a definite 'tempo' of four to the bar. So Wren's dome is no mere enlargement of Bramante but an imaginative extension – just as Bramante was an extension of the antique.

Over and over again, in the seventeenth and eighteenth centuries, this Tempietto idea comes into play – the colonnade surrounding the

34    cylindrical, domed core. Hawksmoor, in his mausoleum at Castle Howard makes it tragic, columns close and forbidding like a palisade, dome deflated, unaspiring; and for base a funereal platform, prostrating itself along the ground. But then look at James Gibbs's

35    Radcliffe Library at Oxford. Is this the same theme? It is. But the columns have re-grouped themselves in pairs, pairs unequally spaced, over a podium which with its pedimented projections accents one set of intervals and under a dome whose buttresses descend emphatically over the other set. Curiously elaborate and sophisticated, it would have delighted a Gonzaga or a Medici and is perhaps slightly absurd for a building whose sole function is to make space for serious books and serious readers in an English university.

Plate 37 shows you another classic invention of Bramante's. It is the palace in Rome which Raphael, the painter, lived in for a time so that it is always called after him. It no longer stands. The main rooms of this palace were at the top. Below was a series of arches let off as shops – a common Roman practice. Bramante has given the lower part the rough but disciplined character of Roman engineering works. To the upper part only he has attached an order, Doric, coupled, on pedestals, the pedestals ranging with the balustrades of the windows. Elementary it may seem to us – a direct prose statement. But, as in the case of the Tempietto, it was new. The Romans had not done this – not quite. It was, once again, an extension of Rome, appropriate to sixteenth-century life. And, once again, this new classic echoes down

42

the centuries to our own. Sansovino brought it to Venice and the Grand Canal. They do not have shops on the Grand Canal; so here the 36 three middle arches of the ground floor become a grand entrance while the side arches are replaced by windows. And, Venice demanding additional height, Sansovino duplicated Bramante's upper storey, arriving at something which faintly but I think deliberately echoes the Roman Colosseum. Then, nearer home, there is the Strand front of Somerset House, a clear descendant of 38 Bramante: date, 1780. And when you are in the Strand, just look across from there to the shop-filled arches and arrogantly bedizened Doric columns of Australia House – Bramante again, in the age of British Imperialism: date, 1911.

Bramante led architecture in Italy to that stage of complete conquest of the antique and complete confidence in extending and adapting it which we call, in all the arts, the High Renaissance. The generation which followed and accepted him included Raphael, the painter who was also on occasion an architect; Baldassare Peruzzi; the younger Antonio da Sangallo; Sansovino, who, as we have seen, brought Bramante's (and incidentally Peruzzi's) ideas to Venice; and Sanmichele who took them to and developed them in Verona. But on none of these names am I going to dwell; if I did it would be a question mostly of trying to define what they owed to Bramante and in what special directions each of them departed. Instead, I want to move on to the next generation after that and talk of Palladio, Andrea Palladio, because we are thinking about architecture as a language and from this point of view it is more rewarding to put Palladio next to Bramante, even though Bramante died three years before Palladio was born. From Bramante to Palladio is an easy step and this is why. Palladio, a miller's son, came up out of obscurity and spent most of his life in a rather provincial little north-Italian town called Vicenza. There, he grew up among a small landowning intelligentsia to whom Rome was a very long way off indeed. They had, as it were, their own belated High Renaissance. When Palladio got to Rome as a young man the first thing which must have struck him was the appalling inadequacy of the only published drawings of the Roman ruins – those of our old friend Serlio, whose book was then fairly new. Palladio no doubt felt that Serlio had only scratched the surface of these studies, had omitted much that was valuable and had never really much conception of those refinements of profile and proportion which were the essence of the antique. So Palladio became a scholar of architecture, the most learned and exact of his time. But he became much more than that. He overtook Bramante's mastery of the grammar of Roman architecture and when opportunities came to him – as they did, thick and fast, in and around Vicenza and later in Venice – he built buildings in which the language of Rome was more eloquent, more articulate, than it had ever been.

22
40

When I say 'more articulate', I mean something quite precise. Let me demonstrate. Look back, first, to the interior of S. Andrea, Mantua, and then turn forward to the interior of Il Redentore, Venice. There is almost exactly a hundred years between the building of these two churches, the first by Alberti, the second by Palladio. You will see that the bay design – that is to say, the repeating unit of piers and arches – is very much the same in both. But Alberti expresses himself only in pilasters, Palladio in half columns. This is what I mean by articulation. In Palladio's church you are much more aware of the order than in Alberti's; and at the east end of the Redentore, Palladio's order becomes perfectly free as it turns round to form an apsidal screen behind the altar. It seems as if Palladio's church *really* is an affair of lofty columns supporting their heavy entablatures: the walls and arches seem merely to fill in between them.

Now look at plate 39, Palladio's Chiericati Palace at Vicenza, an important town house in which the ground floor offers an open colonnade to the public and the first floor has two open balconies so that the walls only come out to the street-front where they enclose the grand saloon in the centre. Again, Palladio makes his orders the dominant factor in the building. In both these buildings – in nearly all Palladio's buildings – you have the sense of his deep love of the orders and his great pride in exhibiting them in his own perfectionist versions. He was resurrecting Rome in Vicenza with even more realism than Bramante had resurrected it in Rome herself.

Now this realism in recalling Rome is only one aspect of Palladio. It happens to be the one that best suits my exposition at the moment. And it is, of course, inseparable from another aspect I have already mentioned: Palladio the archaeologist. Archaeologist is perhaps not quite the right word because Palladio's enquiries into the past were more strongly tinged with imaginative awareness of what might have been than we should think quite proper. Still, call it archaeology. When Palladio investigated the text of Vitruvius or the ruins of Rome his results led him at once to make 'restorations' and these restorations were among the most exciting things in his book – or rather books: I mean the *Four Books of Architecture* (the *Quattro Libri*), published in 1570. The effect of these reconstructions reached far beyond Italy: in fact they were more fertile outside Italy than in and their impact in England was rather specially important. The portico of St Paul's, 45 Covent Garden, by Inigo Jones, for instance, is based on Palladian archaeology. It follows (though with certain expert and sensitive deviations) Palladio's literal interpretation of what Vitruvius tells us 44 about the Tuscan order. Those fine, spreading eaves, those wide-apart columns, are Palladian archaeology.

A hundred years after Inigo Jones, Lord Burlington availed himself of Palladio's archaeology when he built the Assembly Rooms at York. Plates 46 and 47 show just how literally he did so. But this building has significance in another context and I shall return to it later on.

Now in taking Bramante and certain aspects of Palladio together I have been confining myself to the grand simplicities of sixteenth-century Italy, the re-establishment of the Latin of architecture: the orders arrogantly displayed and drilled with absolute conviction. It is just possible, I think, that along with the completeness, the authority, the finality of all this you may have begun to feel a certain uneasiness – not to say boredom. The five orders can, of course, become the most terrific bore. If you do feel a slight uneasiness you are not alone; you are very much with some of the more adventurous and romantic personalities of the generation which followed Bramante, some of the men who were in Rome when he died in 1515, who were still in Rome when Raphael died in 1520 and perhaps still about the place when it was sacked and pillaged by the Imperial troops in 1527. There was at that time a very considerable uneasiness about what the High Renaissance (as we call it now) had achieved. There are signs of an incipient malaise even in some of Raphael's last works; and in the work of one of his pupils, Giulio Romano, there is positive revolt, a romantic dash for freedom.

But I cannot begin to talk about Giulio without explaining the meaning of a word of great significance in classical architecture from this time on – *rustication*. What is rustication? As the word rather implies, it was at first conceived to mean a rough countrified way of laying stones, each particular stone retaining some of the individuality it had when hewn from the quarry. However, this rustic roughness was recognized as having character – artistic possibilities – and it became in due course the subject of extreme sophistication. Already, by the time Serlio was writing his fourth book (published, 1537) rustication had been stylized and systematized. From being just rough it had become highly artificial, cut into geometrical facets. Serlio describes rustication, however, as being fundamentally a mixture of the natural and the artificial – he seems to imply a sort of struggle between the artificer and the forces of nature. This, of course, is a thoroughly romantic idea and in the works of Giulio Romano we can see it at work. Look at the detail, plate 49, of the Palazzo del Tè, the summer palace of the Dukes of Mantua. Here is a very strange performance. You recognize, of course, the Doric order. And the major columns are approximately on the triumphal arch pattern. But the pediment rests not on columns but on brackets emerging from the wall, and the keystone of the arch pushes violently up into the pediment. Everything is a bit uneasy, a bit wrong. Do you notice that in the entablature some of the stones have slipped? And do you notice that these 'slipped' stones occur in exactly the same places on each side of the centre?

What is this all about? That it represents a flight from everything Bramante stood for is pretty obvious. It is irrational, impressionistic. It recalls ruins (especially, of course, in the deliberately dropped stones). It recalls ancient buildings left half-finished. But it has great power and this is very largely because of the dramatic use of rustication. The stones seem to be quarrelling all the time with the highly finished architectural detail. The rough keystones in the two side recesses are forcing a cornice up into the stones above. The keystones of the two round-headed niches are grotesquely too big, that of the centre arch is absurdly small. In patches, here and there, there is no rustication at all and suddenly the wall looks embarrassingly naked.

How serious is all this? Well, I am sure it is not meant to be funny. It is an arrogant protest against rules and, yes, it is poetry; a poetry which has something to do with grottos and with the cult of giants and dwarfs which seems to have haunted the court of Federigo Gonzaga. For us now, the importance of it all is the quantity of sheer invention it contains. Giulio didn't invent rustication (the Romans used it; Brunelleschi used it; Bramante had used it in the House of

Raphael), but Giulio did bring it to a pitch of expressiveness which no one else had dreamed of and from which very few architects after his time failed to benefit. From the Palazzo del Tè, he went on to the Ducal Palace itself and built that unforgettable study in the classical-grotesque, the Cortile della Cavallerizza. And lastly, to complete our glimpse of Giulio, look at his design for a city gateway – a triumphal arch conceived entirely in terms of this same exaggerated toughness. 48 50

The long-term effect of Giulio's inventions was tremendous. Even Palladio, who you might think, from what I have said of him, would be proof against such explosive stuff, borrowed from him in his later palaces. In eighteenth-century England, Newgate Prison had Giulio to thank for its horrific solemnity. And you cannot walk through any commercial centre built up in the nineteenth–twentieth centuries without seeing banks and insurance offices loaded up with rustic devices, many of which have their origin in Mantua. Look at the load carried by London's elected representatives at County Hall. 98 99

But I must end up by introducing you to a much greater revolutionary than Giulio Romano, to the man who really did outrage the authority of the High Renaissance and turn classical architecture into new courses – Michelangelo.

Michelangelo was twenty-five years older than Giulio Romano, but had done no architecture at all when Giulio began the Palazzo del Tè; and his major works nearly all belong to the period after Giulio's death in 1546, when he himself was over seventy. His architecture is a world away from Giulio's. Rustication had almost no interest for him. His walls are smooth and their power is concentrated into tightly bounded surfaces, recessions and projections and moulded elements which are rarely enriched. Michelangelo always insisted that he was not an architect but a sculptor, yet no professed architect has ever had so startling an effect on architecture. Vasari said of him that 'he broke the bonds and chains of a way of working that had become habitual by common usage'. That is, if anything, an understatement; it does scant justice to the positive effects of Michelangelo's inventions, the enormous incentive they supplied.

The 'way of working' mentioned by Vasari was, of course, the way of the High Renaissance masters since Bramante, that is to say, the grammatical approach through a study of Vitruvius, filled out by prolonged observation of the antiquities of Rome. Cornice profiles and the dressings of doors and windows were all designed with reference to antique authority. If an architect's own sensitivity entered into his designs it was involuntary and through chinks in the process of selection from the consecrated sources. Now, on this whole idea of 'authority' Michelangelo turned his back. He was already a sculptor with a mastery of form and material transcending the antique and when he turned to architecture this same power of seeing through the dead, accepted forms to something intensely alive enabled him to transcend, with absolute assurance, the Vitruvian grammar. As Vasari says, rather naïvely, 'he proceeded quite differently in proportion, composition and rules from what others had done following common practice'. He did indeed – quite differently.

Look at plates 53 and 55. Here are two architectural frames or 'aedicules' by two great classical masters. One is by Raphael, a beautifully elegant piece of classical prose at the Palazzo Pandolfini, Florence. Perfect of its kind, but not exactly moving, and nearly every line can be described categorically in Vitruvian terms. The other is by Michelangelo, one of the niche-like recesses in the Medici Chapel at S. Lorenzo. This is almost impossible to describe in words. It has some of the main elements of the Raphael work: pilasters, pediment, architrave, but all are re-invented and full of what a Vitruvian critic would have to call gross and absurd errors. Are the pilasters Doric, or what? What is the sense of those breaks in the curved line of the pediment? And by what rule or precedent does an architrave moulding go sliding up into the tympanum to lean its sharp elbows on a cornice? No, this work is really almost abstract sculpture. It is Michelangelo's personal equivalent of the Vitruvian. It strikes the beholder, perhaps, as strange, even at first unacceptable. But it stays in the memory, this curiously tense, deeply felt creation. No architect – anyway no young and impressionable architect – who visited the Medici Chapel when Michelangelo had done with it could ever feel quite the same about architecture again.

48

*31*

Colonnaded circular temples, including those dedicated to Vesta, were among the most engaging monuments of Roman antiquity. **31** The temple near the Tiber, usually called the Temple of Vesta (but more plausibly assigned to Portumnus) has lost the whole of its entablature. Its exceptionally tall Corinthian columns still assert its nobility of form.

32

## Progeny of the circular temple

The theme was destined to have many variant forms. **32** The earliest derivation was Bramante's Tempietto in the cloister of S. Pietro in Montorio, 1502. **33** Wren's dome of St Paul's, London (1696–1708), raises Bramante's interpretation to the colossal scale of the cathedral over which it presides. **34** Hawksmoor's mausoleum at Castle Howard (1729) is no less derivative but in a wholly different mood. **35** James Gibbs rehandled the theme with elaborated rhythms in his Radcliffe Library at Oxford (1739–40).

33

34

35

36

An innovation of the sixteenth century was the palace front with an order standing over an arched and rusticated lower storey. **37** Bramante's long-since demolished House of Raphael, 1512, shows Doric columns arranged in couples, standing over the piers of the arches in the podium. **36** Sansovino's Palazzo Corner, Venice, 1532, repeats the pattern with variations and adds another storey. **38** Somerset House, London, by Sir William Chambers, 1780, shows a clear descent from Bramante with subtler modelling and perhaps some loss of vigour.

37

**The order on a podium**

38

39

Palladio, who was born three years after Bramante died, brought the classical formulae into play with a wonderful combination of antiquarian learning and artistic invention. It was this developed language which, through Palladio's *Quattro Libri dell'Architettura* (1570), became widely acceptable in the western world. **39** The Palazzo Chiericati, Vicenza, 1551–54, commanding a public square, is both Vitruvian and modern. **40** Palladio's church of Il Redentore, Venice, fulfils the promise of Alberti's S. Andrea, Mantua (*pl. 22*) with a fully articulated Corinthian order.

40

41

41 One of Palladio's boldest grammatical constructions is the west front of S. Giorgio Maggiore, Venice, composed of two interpenetrating temple fronts.

## Palladio and Palladianism

42

42 The Villa Rotonda, Vicenza, 1550–51, views the surrounding countryside from four temple porticos leading to a circular domed hall.
43 Lord Burlington's villa at Chiswick, 1725; one of several houses in England which borrow the forms at the Villa Rotonda.

43

## Palladian archaeology

Palladio's reconstructions of ancient buildings, often imaginative rather than scientific but always structurally plausible, exercised as much influence as his own designs. **44** Palladio's version of the primitive Tuscan order, based on the description of Vitruvius. **45** At St Paul's, Covent Garden, in 1631, Inigo Jones adopted the primitive Tuscan as a gesture combining economy with the radicalism of the reformed church. **46** Palladio's reconstruction of the 'Egyptian Hall' described by Vitruvius. **47** The almost literal replica of Palladio's reconstruction made by Lord Burlington for the Assembly Rooms at York, 1730.

45

46

## Rustication

Rustication is the art of treating masonry in such a way as to give a building, or parts of it, special character or emphasis. The word conveys the idea of roughness, as of stones just hewn from the quarry, but the commonest form, sometimes found in antiquity, is the neat grooving of the joints between the stones. Some Renaissance masters, however, took the idea very much further.

**48** In Giulio Romano's Cortile della Cavallerizza, Mantua, 1538–39, stones of grotesquely contrasting sizes are hacked and tooled in various ways, and the Doric columns are grooved and twisted almost out of recognition.

48

**49** In his Palazzo del Tè, his play with rustication goes to the extent of affected dilapidation and includes a symmetrical arrangement of 'dropped' stones in the entablature, while his drawing for the Porta Citadella, Mantua (**50**), *c.* 1533, is a vigorous rendering of the triumphal arch theme in the rustic mode.

49

50

**51** Serlio devotes a page to types of rustication which he associates with the Tuscan order. **52** An example outside Italy: the Palace of Charles V at Granada, 1527–68.

51

52

## Michelangelo

After Bramante and his followers had restored the classical language, with all its grammatical logic, to the sixteenth century, the equilibrium was at once upset by the most powerful imagination of the age. Michelangelo mastered the architectural prose of the ancients but made out of it a new architectural poetry, the poetry of a sculptor. **53** Every element in this window by Raphael in the Palazzo Pandolfini, Florence, can be described in Vitruvian terms. **55** But to describe this niche by Michelangelo in the Medici Chapel, Florence, 1521–24, would be beyond the Vitruvian vocabulary: its intensity of feeling defies technical description. **54** In Michelangelo's vestibule to the Laurentian Library, Florence, 1525–34, columns retreat irrationally into walls whose negative prominence is perversely emphasized by blind windows.

53

54

56

**56** The Porta Pia, Rome, was designed by Michelangelo in 1562, when he was eighty-nine. It resembles an impressionistic doodle, crammed with alternative ideas, suddenly frozen solid. There are, for instance, alternative pediments (one broken, the other not) with alternative fillings – a tablet and a garland. **57** Such was the magic of Michelangelo's reputation that nearly every detail of this strange creation found an echo somewhere in European architecture. At Arundel House, London, in 1618, Inigo Jones incorporated the pediment-within-pediment idea in an otherwise orthodox gateway.

57

# CHAPTER FOUR

# The Rhetoric of the Baroque

Why was it that the Medici Chapel had such a powerful effect? Well, I do not know. I can only leave those two illustrations to speak for themselves. I suppose it is necessary to feel the conventionality of the Raphael aedicule in order to feel the startling unconventionality of the Michelangelo aedicule. Michelangelo's distortions of the Latin of architecture here are rather like his distortions of the human body in many of his sculptures; only we all know, or think we know, the human body and easily grasp the significance of distortions, while few of us know our architectural Latin very well. Anyway, I think that something of the intensity of Michelangelo's handling of architectural form is inescapable; it does not surely have to be underlined by comparisons and analogies.

Michelangelo's other architectural works have not all this same intense originality of detail – they surprise us in other ways. Look at plate 58, one of the palaces on the Capitoline Hill at Rome. Here Michelangelo is using a very big and quite conventional Corinthian pilaster order. But there are two special things about it. One is that it *is* very big: the pilasters are forty-five feet high and so are going in the direction of Michelangelo's St Peter's, where they become simply  59  colossal – in fact ninety feet high. The other thing is that these pilasters pass through two storeys. The Romans had never done this: in fact the Capitoline palaces are, very roughly, like Roman temples whose sides have been 'filled in' with modern work – walls and windows above, an open storey below. And notice that the upper wall rests on an entablature supported by Ionic columns, two to a bay. This arrangement, this way of making two orders work together to control a two-storey building, was one of Michelangelo's most valuable and liberating inventions.

It is an easy step from the Capitoline palace to Baroque church façades. Many of them (for instance S. Andrea al Quirinale) make use  76  of the Capitoline theme. But these churches are more than a hundred years later than the Capitoline, and I cannot talk about Baroque without first trying to give you some idea what went on in Italian architecture between the time when the double impact of Giulio Romano and Michelangelo was first received in the 1530s and 1540s and the time when the Baroque got into its stride a century later.

There is a name for what went on and it is 'Mannerism'. Mannerism means very much what we mean when we talk of a person being 'mannered' – that is to say, affecting to imitate a type and in doing so showing an artificiality, an affectation of manner. Mannerism is not a style. It is the 'mood' of an age and all sorts of very different things happened while that mood prevailed. For our purpose, which is to consider architecture as a language, what we want to know is the extent to which Mannerism coloured the language and enriched its vocabulary. In plates 60 and 72 are two very famous buildings by Vignola, both of which are always considered outstanding monuments of the age of Mannerism. Take first the

60   Castello Farnese, Caprarola. I must explain at once that the bastion-like features at the corners of the house are the result of the foundations having been laid and the walls partly carried up on another plan by another architect. Apart from these, the main block of the house could be, for all you can see in the photograph, simply an extension of High Renaissance practice – something that Bramante perhaps and Raphael certainly might have composed – though a rather obvious divergence is that the three-arched loggia between the curving steps is rusticated (rather gently) in the manner of Giulio Romano.

61   But now look at the engraving from Vignola's book. This is a detail of the main entablature at Caprarola. It is not quite like any of the entablatures in our plates 1–4 though it has something in common with Serlio's rather ugly version of the Composite, and this in fact is the clue. Serlio's source for his Composite was the pilastered top storey of the Colosseum: the top storey at Caprarola, with its pilasters, is based on this same theme. But Vignola has very brilliantly invented an entablature which is, at one and the same time, nicely in scale with the pilaster order below it and big and bold enough to form a crowning feature for the whole mass of the building. It is a departure from the strict grammar of the antique – a departure in the direction of inventive modelling, of designing a façade as a pattern in light and shade, a pattern through which runs a *play* of meaning rather than any precise series of statements.

64

This way of putting it may be clearer when applied to a more thoroughly Mannerist façade; so turn to the second Vignola building I mentioned – the church of the Gesù, the principal church of the Jesuit order in Rome. This is a huge church (photographs always make it look too small) with a huge west front in two pilastered storeys, both of them Corinthian. If you look at this building carefully and try to spell out its architecture in High Renaissance terms you soon get into difficulties. There is no clear repetitive rhythm. Surfaces advance and recede in a baffling way, and at one point on the ground storey one pilaster seems to be partly tucked in behind another. Obviously the whole thing is meant to be received as a broad piece of architectural modelling within which, as I said before, a certain play of meaning resides.

72

It is important to understand these products of the age of Mannerism because their effect reached a very long way. The early Victorians, for instance, rediscovered Mannerist architecture (though they did not call it that – they just called it Italian). They rediscovered Mannerist architecture as something exactly suited to themselves. It seemed to release them from the cold pedantry of the classical revivals and it had what they liked to call 'character'. Most of the big, black banks and many of the more ornate warehouses in places like Manchester, Liverpool and Leeds are thoroughly 'Mannerist' in inspiration, interesting now mainly because for us they reflect the Victorian image so sharply. But occasionally the artistry of the original Mannerists shines through, as it does in the work of our one Victorian classical architect of international calibre, Charles Robert Cockerell. The little drawing, plate 62, shows how Cockerell drew from Caprarola most of what he needed for an insurance office in the City of London. Plate 64 shows, in parenthesis, what somebody else made of Cockerell fifty years later – a regular fruit-salad of Mannerist *and* Baroque material, a piece of professional showmanship exactly suited to the mood of *fin-de-siècle* critics who, for a few years, thought the Chartered Accountants Institute the most wonderful modern building in London.

Cockerell is worth much more attention than this kind of thing and for sheer wit and invention in the handling of Mannerist themes there is no building in Britain quite like his Ashmolean building in Oxford. Cockerell saw with the eyes of the Italian Mannerists but saw far more; and the Greek detail of which, as an archaeologist, he was a

63

master wonderfully enriches the Mannerist idiom of Vignola, whose famous cornice – re-profiled – you will at once recognize.

In our next six plates (66–71), Mannerism is shown penetrating in
66 another direction altogether. The palace at Lucca is a charming work by the Florentine Mannerist architect (who was also a sculptor), Ammanati. It is very tight and tense with any amount of 'modelling': sunk panels, raised panels, raised panels within sunk panels and over the haunches of the arch on the ground floor a deliberate absurdity – two Ionic capitals carved as if in suspension, or as if they were part of a thin film of architecture partly cut away to reveal the arch. This sculptural attitude to façades, which derives ultimately from Michelangelo, is reflected again (but perhaps even more so) in the courtyard of the Palazzo Marino, Milan. This is a little square
67 courtyard – three arches to each side – which few visitors to Milan ever bother to look at, though it is plumb in the centre of the city. The curious thing about this, a work of Galeazzo Alessi, is that, above the Doric order on the ground floor, with its very much contracted entablature, nearly everything has got turned into sculpture – or, rather, the architecture is put in in outline and the surfaces are filled with figure-sculpture, animal masks, swags and festoons of fruit and flowers. Instead of an upper order there are 'terms', pedestals narrow at the base and widening to human busts at the top; between these 'terms' are niches containing figures; between the arches are elaborate panels containing sculpture in relief; and so on. All very theatrical and probably, indeed, of theatrical origin. Now this kind of architectural décor travelled very easily – anyway it travelled north very easily; furthermore it lent itself to the making of highly attractive engraved plates such as you see reproduced in plates 70 and 71. These are by the Fleming, Vredeman de Vries, and the German, Wendel Dietterlin, respectively, and they show the form in which the architecture of Mannerism reached – among other places – Elizabethan England. In
69 fact, Wollaton Hall is decorated very largely with quotations from De Vries. And although Dietterlin's frightfully intricate designs were not often copied in England, his book was so well known that Elizabethan and Jacobean ornament became generically known, in the seventeenth and eighteenth centuries, as 'ditterling' ornament.

All this is taking us to the far outside edge of our subject and I am not inviting you for one moment to consider Wollaton Hall as an important manifestation of the classical language; it may be important for a great deal else, but not for that. To copy De Vries was to copy quite pretty paper patterns containing only a skin-deep appreciation of the kind of classical designing which this book is about.

So let us get back to the centre of the stage. Two other west fronts quite obviously derive from that of the Gesù. If you compare S. Susanna, in Rome, with the Gesù you will be struck at once by two things. First, that it is much more compact; it insists definitely on a vertical rectangle, and the scrolls over the aisles, which swing out in the Gesù, are here drawn firmly in to help the vertical stress. Second, you will feel, I think, that whereas the pattern of pilasters in the Gesù façade is diffuse, in S. Susanna the arrangement of columns and pilasters is unmistakably designed to bring your attention to the centre and indeed to the central door. Now this comparison has often been made and is as handy a comparison as any to explain the difference between Mannerist and Baroque architecture – S. Susanna is Baroque. But just to show how careful you have to be with these terms, look now at a third church – the Val de Grâce, built in Paris fifty years later than S. Susanna. Mannerist? Baroque? Well, let us see. It has not the diffuseness and ambiguity of the Gesù; but neither has it the force and decision of S. Susanna. Nor is it merely something between the two. It has a character of its own. It is relaxed and harmonious and the gradual articulation of the ground-floor order from pilaster to column-in-the-round seems to breathe a truer classical spirit than anything in the other two buildings. Mannerist? Baroque? No; neither. It is a personal interpretation, by a Frenchman, of the Gesù theme; and the interpretation belongs to a phase in French art which has classical standards of its own, the standards of Poussin, of Racine – and of Mansart, the architect of this church.

It is impossible to dodge the occasional embarrassment of these generalizing expressions: 'High Renaissance', 'Mannerist', 'Baroque', and so on. We cannot escape using them and in fact I have used one for the title of this chapter, in calling it 'The Rhetoric of the Baroque'. Baroque is nearly always rhetorical, in the sense of grandiloquent, contrived, persuasive oratory; and if we are talking about architecture as a sort of language, this is a useful qualification of some of the greater buildings of the seventeenth century – the ones we mostly have in mind when we use the word 'Baroque'. And I am going to conclude this chapter by considering three such works. First, the Piazza of St

*72, 73*

*75*

Peter's, Rome, by Bernini. Second, the east front of the Palais du Louvre, Paris, by Le Vau, Perrault and Le Brun. Third, Blenheim Palace, near Oxford, by Vanbrugh and Hawksmoor. In case anybody should want to ask me: 'Are you quite sure all these are pure Baroque?', let me say at once that the answer is 'No, of course I am not sure.' For one thing there is no such category as 'pure Baroque' – just because there is a word, it does not mean there is a pure essence to match it. For another thing, while it could certainly be proved beyond reasonable doubt that these three buildings are entitled to the appellation Baroque, it could be shown with equal certainty that there are things about each which might *dis*qualify them in some contexts. So let us not bother. Let us just look at the buildings themselves and see what they have to say to us.

*79, 80* Bernini designed the Piazza before St Peter's as a huge enclosed forecourt. As such you see it in the air-view, taken before the demolitions of Mussolini's time. It is a forecourt, not an 'approach': a forecourt, an enclosed space, an atrium, built with the specific purpose of accommodating great gatherings to receive the blessing of the Pope. Apart from the two straight corridors attaching themselves to the façade of the church, it consists of one immense oval space partly defined by two curved regiments of columns: columns fifty feet high and standing four deep. There are here in all 280 free-standing, fifty-foot-high columns, probably the most imposing assembly of columns in the world. And the columns are – what? Doric? Well, yes; except that they have Tuscan bases and are a trifle taller than the conventional Doric and that they carry an entablature which is not Doric at all but more or less Ionic. In other words, for this particular occasion, Bernini has taken the law into his own hands and designed his own order – an order fusing the soldierly dignity of the Doric with the elegance of the Ionic. It is a curiously memorable order. One remembers it, inevitably, as Doric (because of the capitals); but as a Doric with a personality entirely its own.

I want to make it clear what a tremendous impression these colonnades make. Remember that the columns are repeated three times behind what you see in the photograph, so that when you are inside the colonnades, on the route taken sometimes by great processions, these ascending cylinders press round you like forest trees. The sun strikes through as it may; and from this ceremonious forest you look across the Piazza to another, as large and as deep. Then notice how each of those two giant crescents, whose own rhythm could so easily run away with them, is steadied by columns standing out at the ends and again, in coupled pairs, at the centre – sentinels. It is a marvellous performance and, of course, the opportunity was marvellous, and unique: the opportunity to build a structure of this size and to build it entirely of columns. The opportunity has, so far as I know, never occurred again; it has only been envied.

Now a palace is a very different thing; when we turn to the Louvre  81 in Paris we see another colonnade but one whose existence has had to be contrived as part of a royal residence. The designing of this east front was one of the great episodes of European architectural history. The rest of the Louvre had been built over a period of a hundred years, and Colbert, Louis XIV's minister, was determined that the east front should be the culminating success of the whole. All the leading French architects were asked for designs and some famous Italians, too – including Bernini, who visited Paris in great state and whose design was accepted. But it was not built. In the end, the work was entrusted to three men: Le Vau, the King's First Architect; Le Brun, his First Painter; and a physician of wide scientific attainments, Claude Perrault – and it is always supposed that Perrault's was the most original and innovating mind of the three.

The result is spectacular. Never had any Italian master succeeded – or perhaps ever had occasion to seek success – in the exposition of Roman temple architecture on this scale in combination with the purposes of a palace. But the first thing that strikes one about the Louvre is, of course, this Corinthian colonnade of fully articulated Roman columns. The columns are in pairs. We have seen this arrangement before, in Bramante's House of Raphael; it is a good way  37 of securing the wide intercolumniation you need for windows. But Bramante's columns were against a wall. At the Louvre the inner wall is, for part of the way, set right back so that the columns stand out as if they were indeed part of a temple colonnade. But taking the whole length of this façade together, you will see that, although the colonnade is an immediately striking and dramatic element in it, it is not the only factor which makes for its success. This is due to the handling of the order as a whole – its integration with the building, its control of the building. And how is this managed? In two long stretches, as we have just seen, the order has its independence. In the centre feature, however, it comes a pace forward and carries a pediment; and here the columns are backed by a solid wall – a wall, incidentally, which has an arch in it, covering the main entrance, and which (above the arch) is splendidly decorated with low-relief sculpture. Then in the end blocks (pavilions the French call them and so, mostly, do we), the wall comes further forward and the order, with the same intercolumniation as in the colonnade, turns itself into pilasters. But in compensation, as it were, in the (subtly widened) middle intercolumniation in these end pavilions is a recess where the wall goes back to the plane of the wall in the centre pavilion, and moreover contains a round-arched window echoing the entrance arch in the centre. Follow this carefully in the illustration, because the Louvre is a wonderful example of the 'play' of a classical order in controlling a very long frontage not merely without monotony but with wit and grace and aesthetic logic. I will only add, concerning the Louvre, that the carved ornaments have crispness and delicacy of a kind which is peculiarly French and which accounts for the extraordinary vitality of this building, which on a brilliant spring morning looks like the newest, freshest thing you ever saw in your life.

82, 83 And now, lastly, another palace, but utterly different from the Louvre – Blenheim Palace. Not, this time, one long façade with subtle variations of plane but a building of many parts, deploying this way and that, advancing, receding; not one long serene skyline but a silhouette in violent motion. Blenheim Palace, built by Queen Anne for the Duke of Marlborough as a reward for his services to the nation and at the same time as a monument to British military glory, was the joint work of Vanbrugh and Hawksmoor. It is easily one of the most complex classical buildings in all Europe. Vanbrugh fused in his work two very different influences. One was what you would expect – a passionate love of Roman architecture and all that the great masters and theorists had done with it (in that he had the fullest possible support from his colleague, Hawksmoor). The other influence was an unexpected one for his time: Vanbrugh had a strong feeling for medieval castles and for those most daring of all English buildings, the
69 great towered and turreted houses of Elizabethan and Jacobean times. At Blenheim these two influences merge in the exciting and apparently chaotic result you see. But Blenheim is not chaotic: it is most beautifully and logically put together.

Take first those two towers, left and right, heavily rusticated and crowned by a mass of piers and pinnacles. There are in fact four of these towers. They mark the four corners of a rectangle: they pin Blenheim down to the soil. These towers have no classical order. The rest of the house has: it is controlled by two orders – a fifty-foot Corinthian and a Doric half that height, and those two orders play a sort of counterpoint between, into and out from the towers. The centre block of the house is Corinthian – fully articulated columns in the portico, pilasters on either flank. The Doric order is, as it were, hiding in this block; it is just detectable in the sides of the ground-floor windows: three each side of the portico. But in the wings, out it comes. There is a double beat, then it wheels round. Another double beat: it turns, enters the towers – it disappears. Then out it marches from the near side of each tower, marches forward till it is returned as a formal entry with steps inside and a flourish of arms above. That is very roughly the layout of this architectural manoeuvre, this still choreography. There is a great deal more to Blenheim than that. There is the way the verticals of the portico shoot up through the pediment and then run back to meet the gable of the hall – a truly dramatic, *just* not melodramatic, invention. There is the way the Corinthian order penetrates the building and comes out to a different sort of portico on the park side. But Vanbrugh and Hawksmoor could never have made what they did of Blenheim without knowing – through engravings – what Bernini and his predecessors had done, on just about double the scale, at St Peter's half a century before. Compare Blenheim with the little air-view of St Peter's; the Doric 79 wings of Blenheim with Bernini's colonnades; the giant order at 80 Blenheim with Michelangelo's giant pilasters at St Peter's. 59

Well, there are three buildings which, I believe, demonstrate with peculiar brilliance the 'rhetoric' of the Baroque. Yes, I think, 'rhetoric' is the key word. These buildings use the classical language of architecture with force and drama in order to overcome our resistance and persuade us into the truth of what they have to tell us – whether it is about the invincible glory of British arms, the paramount magnificence of Louis XIV, or the universal embrace of the Roman Church.

## Michelangelo and the giant order

The 'giant' order is one which rises from the ground or from a low base and ascends through two or more storeys. A multi-storey building may thus assume the scale of a great temple. Each individual storey nevertheless retains its own scale, which may be expressed by a secondary order of appropriate dimensions. This combination of orders at two scales was one of Michelangelo's innovations.

**58** In the twin palaces on the Capitoline Hill, Rome, Michelangelo's giant
Corinthian order embraces two storeys, while a subsidiary Ionic gives expression
and support to the intermediate floor. **59** The giant Corinthian pilasters of the
apses of St Peter's, Rome, are 90 feet high.

60

## Mannerism

'Mannerism' is the art of the *tour-de-force*, of problems undertaken for their novelty and curiosity. **60** The Castello Farnese, Caprarola, by Vignola, 1559–64, is in some respects a High Renaissance creation, but the approach is an exciting new adventure. **61** The main cornice of the Castello Farnese, ingeniously fusing the Corinthian with the Doric, was one of Vignola's most effective inventions; a plate from his *Regola*, 1563. **62** C.R. Cockerell's Sun Assurance Building, Threadneedle Street (1841; demolished) borrowed liberally from the upper storey of the Castello. **63** Cockerell adapted the Vignolesque cornice again, rather differently, at the Ashmolean Museum, Oxford – a building in which Mannerist artifice and Greek archaeology are combined with great subtlety. **64** A later Victorian, John Belcher, built the Chartered Accountants Institute, 1890; here the authority of the

61

62

63

order surrenders to an ebullience of sculpture and clever detailing. **65** Sir Edwin Lutyens plays the Mannerist game in his Midland Bank, Poultry, London, where Doric pilasters vanish into the rustication, their presence signalled only by emerging caps and bases.

64

65

66

67

## The Mannerist explosion

Mannerism was not a 'style' but the 'mood' of an age. Its manifestations in Italy were infinitely varied and some of them travelled across Europe. **66** The Palazzo Provinciale, Lucca, by Bartolommeo Ammanati, 1577, teases the eye with a subtle play of recession and relief – sunk panels, raised panels, raised panels within sunk panels, and so on. **67** In the Palazzo Marino, Milan, by Galeazzo Alessi, 1558,

68

69

decorative carving takes over almost completely from the orders. **68** The French classicism of Pierre Lescot in the Square Court of the Louvre, Paris, 1546, is strongly tinged with Mannerism. **69** When Mannerism reached Britain it had crystallized into the style we call 'Elizabethan', deriving mostly from Flemish engravers; Wollaton Hall, Nottingham, by Robert Smythson, 1580–88, is a famous example. **70, 71** Two plates from books of designs that influenced northern artists: De Vries's Corinthian order (Antwerp, 1577) and Wendel Dietterlin's 'terms' (Nuremburg, 1594–98).

70

71

In the sixteenth century, an arrangement of orders in two storeys with scrolls in the angles became the typical church façade all over Catholic Europe. Variations on this model are infinite. **72** Vignola's façade of the church of the Gesù, Rome, with its ingeniously complex rhythms, is the great Mannerist prototype. **73** At S. Susanna, Rome, by Carlo Maderna, 1597, the Gesù theme is rendered more compactly, with decisive vertical stress, foreshadowing the Baroque.

## The orders in church façades

**74** By the time Martino Longhi designed the front of SS. Vincenzo ed Anastasio, Rome, in 1646, Baroque rhetoric had given an altogether new direction to Italian church design. **75** Meanwhile, in France, classical balance was retained in the distribution of the familiar elements; the church of the Val de Grâce, Paris, begun by François Mansart in 1645 and completed by Lemercier.

*74*

*75*

The two great masters of the Baroque transformed the classical language in ways
undreamt of by the Renaissance but to which parallels may be found in some late
Roman architecture.

## Bernini and Borromini

**76** The façade of Bernini's S. Andrea al Quirinale, Rome, 1658–70, develops from the thought of Michelangelo. It is like a single bay of the Capitoline Palace (*pl. 58*) in which the Ionic order is set in motion, circuiting the oval form of the church and then swinging out through the giant Corinthian pilasters to make a porch. **77** Borromini's façade of S. Carlo alle Quattro Fontane, Rome, 1665–67, has two orders superimposed, each with a subsidiary order on the Capitoline principle, but on a curving plan. **78** The interior of the church rises from a system of curves struck from points in a complex geometric pattern.

77

78

81

The Baroque age was an age of palaces, providing opportunities for extravagant architectural expression unknown since the days of the cathedrals. **81** The east front of the Louvre, Paris, by Le Vau, Perrault and Le Brun, 1667–70. The five-fold division of the façade is specifically French, though the idea of coupled columns on a high podium goes back to Bramante. **82** Blenheim Palace, built between 1705 and 1724 by Sir John Vanbrugh and Nicholas Hawksmoor. Compared with the Louvre, Blenheim is picturesque and mobile – an affair of contrasting masses through which a major Corinthian and a subsidiary Doric order perform a strong counterpoint.

82

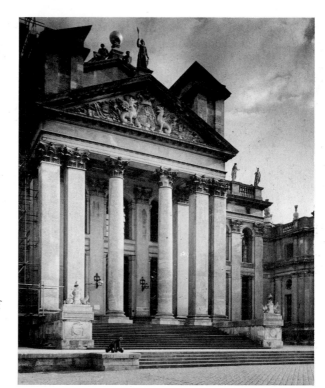

## Two palaces

**83** A closer view of Blenheim brings out the dramatic play of columns and pilasters.

84

85

## Baroque in Venice, Piedmont, Sicily

Each region of Italy had its Baroque masters, interpreting moods and traditions in the new rhetorical spirit. **84** S. Maria della Salute, Venice, begun by Baldassare Longhena in 1631 and often thought of as wildly picturesque, is in fact a highly intellectual design. Built on an octagon plan, the 'triumphal arch' entry forecasts the bay design of the interior so that scenic continuity is achieved. **85** The Superga at Turin (Piedmont) is another intellectual essay in the combination of octagon, drum and dome, owing more, however, to the Roman school. The architect was Filippo Juvarra, 1717–31.

86

**86** Guarini, inspired by the geometrical exercises of Borromini, evolved interiors of such restless contradiction as that of S. Lorenzo, Turin, 1668, where the Palladian motif plays convex against concave in the lateral chapels as well as carrying the piers of the dome. **87** Late Baroque in Sicily produced this volatile interpretation of Vignola's Gesù theme in the façade added to the ancient cathedral of Syracuse in 1728–57.

87

Piedmontese Baroque influence found its way into Germany and led to the creation of churches of wonderful freedom. The orders, divested of the solemnity of the antique, move in a new choreographic harmony, while never betraying the essential logic of the classical language. **88** Die Wies, by Domenikus Zimmermann, 1745–54, uses coupled columns of square section so that a firm line is continued from floor to vault and penetrates the ethereal Rococo decoration.

88

**89** Balthasar Neumann's pilgrimage church of Vierzehnheiligen, 1744, is planned on a series of three ovals, the centre oval rising through a giant Corinthian order to an elliptical vault over the shrine. **90** The façade of St John Nepomuk, Munich, by the brothers Asam, 1733–46, owes much to Bernini and Borromini (see *pls 76 and 77*). The architecture dissolves into plaster sculpture by Egid Asam.

89

90

# CHAPTER FIVE

# The Light of Reason – and of Archaeology

The use of the classical language of architecture has implied, at all times when it has risen to high eloquence, a certain philosophy. You cannot use the orders lovingly unless you love them; and you cannot love them without persuading yourself that they embody some absolute principle of truth or beauty. Belief in the fundamental authority of the orders has taken various forms, the simplest being in these terms: Rome was the greatest; Rome knew best. The sheer veneration of Rome is the clue to much in our civilization. It is a veneration we cannot easily share ourselves because we know too much about Rome and do not always like what we know; and also because we know far more than has ever been known before of other civilizations which ministered to the successes which Rome achieved. But to understand the mind of the fifteenth and sixteenth centuries we must, in this respect, be simple. There is a beautiful story told by Burckhardt of an occasion in 1485, when it was announced that the corpse of a Roman lady, in perfect preservation, had been discovered in an ancient sarcophagus. The corpse was taken to the Palazzo dei Conservatori and as the news spread people thronged to see this marvel. The Roman lady, her mouth and eyes half open, the colour still in her cheeks, was 'more beautiful', says a contemporary, 'than can be said or written and were it said or written, it would not be believed by those who had not seen her'. Of course, the thing was a fake. But the emotion was not. If the lady was Roman, people knew she must be beautiful beyond anything that any living person had ever seen.

That touching and unreasoning faith in Roman excellence belongs mostly to the fifteenth century. It comes back with incredible force in some of the paintings of Mantegna in which senators, consuls, lictors *23* and centurions stand ready to re-enact their parts within an ambience of superb and glittering monuments.

But the simplicity of that faith made it vulnerable. If it inspired action, it also challenged enquiry and criticism; and criticism, while knowing and accepting the fact that Rome was best and greatest, demanded to know why? Why was Rome the fount of all goodness in architecture? One answer was, because all educated people everywhere agreed on the incomparable beauty of Roman architecture; but that merely begged the question. Another answer was that it enshrined certain mathematical rules to which all beauty was accountable; but that was not easy to prove. A third answer – and a much more profound one – was that Roman architecture has descended, through the Greeks, from the most primitive epoch of human history and was thus possessed of a sort of natural rightness, was, indeed, almost a work of nature. Vitruvius was invoked to support this view. He taught that the Doric order developed from a timber prototype and from this it was argued that the original temples had had tree-trunks for columns and were thus derived from the primitive forests. A curious allusion to this belief occurs in some of the columns in the cloisters of S. Ambrogio, Milan, designed by 93 Bramante, where the shafts of the stone columns have the stumps of sawn-off branches carved on them.

But this question of 'why?' did not really worry anybody very much till the seventeenth century, and then it was not in Italy but in France that the questioners appeared. It was natural, I suppose, that a critical spirit should emerge not in the homeland of classical architecture, Italy, but in a country where it had been absorbed and adapted and where it displaced the most intellectual of all medieval building traditions. Anyway, it was in France, about the middle of the seventeenth century, that questions began to be asked about the true nature of the orders and the way they should be used in modern buildings. The 'natural rightness' of the orders was accepted and the first concern of French critics was to ensure their purity and integrity. The new call to order came in a series of books. First, there was the famous *Parallèle*, the *Parallel of the Ancient Architecture with the Modern*, by Roland Fréart, which contains a minute comparison of the orders as found in antiquity and as interpreted by the theorists from Serlio onwards. Fréart pleads for rigorous selective purity. Then came the leading architect of the Louvre, Claude Perrault, with his beautiful and searchingly annotated edition of Vitruvius; likewise his treatise on the orders – the treatise from which I have borrowed plate 4 as being perhaps the most elegant of all engraved presentations of the orders. And then, in 1706, followed a more remarkable book than any of these, a book by a French abbé, the Abbé Cordemoy. On the face of it, Cordemoy's *Nouveau Traité*, his *New Treatise on the whole of Architecture*, seems to be just another critical review of the orders, tending in the same direction as his predecessors. But it is far more than that. Cordemoy wants not only to liberate the orders from every kind of distortion and affectation; he wants to get rid of the whole business of using the orders ornamentally, to get rid of what he calls, rather effectively, 'architecture in relief': pilasters, half columns, three-quarter columns, attached columns, ornamental pediments, pedestals, attic storeys, the lot. His approach is a sort of Primitive Methodism, stripping away all the elaborate linguistics of architecture, all the mystery and drama, all the brilliant play of the Italian masters, and making the orders speak their own original functional language – no more, no less.

This approach was all very fine and much in line with French thought of the period; it was all very *rational* (which, of course, was the point); however, it did not really work even in theory because the orders themselves, as found in Rome, are by no means primitive, by no means functional but, on the contrary, highly stylized. And it was left for another French abbé, the Jesuit Laugier, nearly fifty years later, to announce a theory which really did upset the architectural apple-cart and shift the basis of architectural thought for a century to come. Perhaps more than a century; because I am not sure that he may not justly be called the first modern architectural philosopher.

Now, the established hypothesis of all architectural theorists was that architecture had originated when primitive man built himself a primitive hut. From the hut he went on to the temple and, refining continually on the temple formula, he invented the timber version of the Doric and then copied it in stone. The other orders followed. That was the theory and everybody accepted it. But what nobody had done was to think at all concretely about the primitive hut; and this is what Laugier did. He visualized it. He visualized it as a structure consisting of upright posts, cross beams and a pitched roof – much what you see in the allegorical frontispiece to his book. This, he declared, was the ultimate image of architectural truth, 'the model' (to use his own words) 'upon which all the magnificences of architecture have been imagined'.

Here, for the first time, the basis of authority of the orders was undermined – displaced by something else, by an image of their own hypothetical prototype, which is a functional, a rational prototype. Not that Laugier wanted to banish the orders; on the contrary, he believed that further orders might well be invented. But he wanted architects to use them with the same sense of constructional truth as the posts and beams in the primitive hut. He agreed with Cordemoy that all 'architecture in relief' must go, but he went further in wanting even walls to go. For Laugier, the ideal building consisted entirely of columns – columns carrying beams, carrying a roof.

This may, on the face of it, seem mildly funny; though to us in the late-twentieth century, surrounded by brand-new buildings consisting of reinforced-concrete columns with nothing but glass diaphragms between them, it should not seem funny so much as grandly prophetic. Anyway, in 1753, no *architect* could have proposed anything so crazy as the abolition of walls. But Laugier was not an architect; he was a philosopher and he was dealing in abstractions. He knew, of course, that walls could not be and would not be abolished, but he was establishing a principle of architectural beauty and that principle, he believed, had been revealed to him as quite necessarily an affair of columns. And it is not at all difficult to be with him in this. Look. A single column is just, well, a point on a plan; or rather, a very small circle on a plan – it gives you the module of an order but nothing more. But two columns give you at once an inter-columniation, therefore a rhythm, and there, with the module, you have the germ of a whole building. The principle is as logically valid today as it was two hundred and thirty years ago.

But what effect did Laugier's book, his *Essai sur l'Architecture*, have in 1753? In France it was devoured; in England and in Germany translations appeared within two years. It was discussed and attacked, digested or rejected all over Europe. In actual building, I think it is fair to say that any fresh, innovating work after about 1755 is certain either to be coloured by Laugier's views or to show a positive rejection of them. The building which embodies his principles in the most spectacular degree is the Panthéon in Paris. The Panthéon is now no longer a church but it was begun as one, dedicated to St Genevieve. The architect was Jacques-Germain Soufflot. Soufflot was not exactly a disciple of Laugier's but his own ideas on architectural principles ran close to Laugier's and were probably inflected by them. If you look at the exterior of the Panthéon, you may, I am afraid, be rather baffled by the fact that, contrary to everything Laugier

95

advocated, it consists almost entirely of wall. But if you look carefully you will see grey oblong patches in the walls; and these are filled-in windows; Soufflot's intention, in fact, was more window than wall but his factor of safety proved too low: the windows had to be blocked. The interior is more to the point, though here again, unintended masonry had to be introduced to assure stability. Still, Soufflot's intention is perfectly clear and you feel it today the moment you enter that brittle and coldly exquisite building. He was trying to    *96* build a church in which the order, expressed only in the round, only in independent, cylindrical shafts, not only looked very beautiful but actually did the whole work of carrying the roof. He very nearly succeeded.

Now this is a very long way from another church I described earlier – Palladio's Redentore in Venice, where I made a special point    *40* of the *articulation* of the orders. If Palladio made a virtue of articulation, Soufflot made it quintessential. To put these two churches side by side is to see exactly the difference in ideals between the mid-sixteenth century and the mid-eighteenth. Palladio was trying, above all things, to be truly Roman. Soufflot was trying to be something altogether more philosophical – trying to reach the truth behind Rome, the combined structural and aesthetic truth which the orders, in their origin, could be supposed to have embodied.

The Panthéon is the first major building which can be called neo-classical – 'neo-classical' being the expression which has come to be used for architecture which, on the one hand, tends towards the rational simplification advocated by Cordemoy and Laugier and, on the other hand, seeks to present the orders with the utmost antiquarian fidelity. Reason and archaeology are the two complementary elements which make neo-classicism and which differentiate it from the Baroque. Or do they? Once again I must warn you against giving too exact a meaning to these labels. Just think back to one of the major Baroque works I described in the previous chapter – Bernini's Piazza in front of St Peter's. What, you may say,    *79, 80* could possibly be truer to Laugier's ideal than those giant crescents consisting wholly of independent columns, innocent of all modelling and enrichment. Yes, indeed. As so often happens, the expression of a new ideal had involuntarily presented itself, on one particular occasion, fully fledged, long before it occurred to anybody to formulate the new ideal in words.

93

Something of this sort happened also in English architecture even earlier and in a peculiarly striking way. Look at plate 45 – Inigo Jones's church of St Paul, Covent Garden. It was built in 1631, but if it is not pure neo-classicism I do not know what is. It is a study in the primitive, based on Vitruvius's description of the Tuscan. That fine, spreading roof, those massive wide-spaced columns are almost pure archaeology, *and* about as basically structural as you can get – in fact, well on the way to the primitive hut. A hundred years later, but still well before Laugier's formulation of the new theory, the English were acknowledging Jones's leadership in this direction, one perhaps somewhat over-enthusiastic critic of 1734 describing the Covent Garden church as 'without a rival, one of the most perfect pieces of architecture that the art of man can produce'. If one is in sympathy with the neo-classical ideal one can see what he meant. And this was written only a year or two after Lord Burlington had paid *his* respects to Vitruvian archaeology by building the Assembly Rooms at York, a perfect reconstruction of the 'Oecus Aegyptius' or Egyptian Hall, a Vitruvian model illustrated from Palladio's woodcut.

I do not suppose that Laugier had heard of either of these buildings, but Soufflot obviously knew something of English architecture because he took St Paul's dome as his model for the dome of the Panthéon. You can judge for yourself whether you think the imitation an entire success. To my mind, the narrower inter-columniation of the Panthéon and the elimination of the solid piers in every fourth bay result in a loss of gravity: the Panthéon dome spins rather too airily over the rectangles of the cross-shaped structure below. Soufflot, no doubt, thought he was purifying Wren's design – getting rid of what Cordemoy would have called 'architecture in relief' and seizing only the essentials.

The actual impact of Laugier on English architecture is another story and an important one. The English already had, as we have just seen, a strong tradition of architectural puritanism, appearing first in Inigo Jones, cropping up again and again, even sometimes in Wren and Hawksmoor, and implicit in the English eighteenth-century addiction to Palladio. But perhaps the very fact that the English had this rather puritanical attitude to architecture made them reluctant to go all the way with Laugier. Besides, the English were, under the skin, incurably romantic; and if the rationalism of Laugier pulled in one direction, the wildly irrational inventions of the great architectetcher, Giambattista Piranesi, pulled in another. The imagination of Piranesi was irresistible. Look at plate 97, one of Piranesi's famous prison scenes – a cavernous perspective of Roman arches, chipped and scarred, dripping with horror, and rusticated more wildly than anything at Mantua. An architect could hardly, you would think, have *both* Laugier and Piranesi for his heroes.

And yet that is very much what some English architects did: George Dance, for instance, whose Newgate Prison is obviously in the mood of Piranesi but some of whose other works are just as clearly influenced by Laugier. The establishment, on the whole, was against Laugier. Sir William Chambers, the author of the one great English eighteenth-century treatise on architecture, objected both to the thesis of the primitive hut and to the sweeping elimination of everything except columns in the round. And yet in the plate in Chambers's book where he illustrates the development of the Doric order are two versions of the primitive hut which must surely have been sketched after a reading of Laugier.

Whatever the actual effect of Laugier's thought in England, the idea of primitivism, of searching back to the true, untainted sources of architectural beauty, certainly prevailed in England, and it had two main results. One of these was the Greek Revival. The other was the peculiar, idiosyncratic primitivism of Sir John Soane.

The Greek Revival is something in which England played a very special part. Till the middle of the eighteenth century Greek architecture was something of a mystery. Everybody knew that the Romans had got their architecture from the Greeks and if it was a question of looking for 'untainted sources' Greece was obviously the place to look. But nobody ever went to Greece. It was a long way off; it was part of the Ottoman Empire and neither an easy nor a safe place for the Western traveller. However, in 1751 two Englishmen, James Stuart and Nicholas Revett, set out for Athens; they came back three years later and in 1762 the first volume of their book, containing accurate measured drawings of Greek buildings, was published. A Frenchman, Le Roy, forestalled them with a more pictorial book in 1758, but Stuart and Revett became the acknowledged authorities.

When people saw, for the first time, accurate representations of the Parthenon and the Theseion – the major examples of the Greek Doric order of the age of Pericles – what did they think of them? Were they coarser and cruder than Roman Doric, because earlier in date; or were

*98*

*94*

*100*

they purer because nearer the source? It all depended on what one was looking for. Some saw them as one thing, some as another. You see, Greek Doric *is* squatter and more massive than the Roman. On the other hand its profiles are more tense and subtle. Some latitude of interpretation was inevitable. The first Greek Doric buildings built in England were built more or less as curiosities, exotic souvenirs, in the form of temples and porches on gentlemen's estates. But about the turn of the century the conviction that the Greek Doric – and Greek Ionic and Greek Corinthian – were in all ways purer and better than their Roman counterparts had won the day, and the Greek Revival proper had started. There were now not five orders to choose from but eight: the five Roman orders established long ago by Serlio, and the three Greek orders which could be extracted from Stuart and Revett. The Revivalists, of course, confined themselves to these.

The Greek Revival, which started in England, eventually manifested itself all over Europe and quickly spread to America. It lasted for about thirty years and I do not think anybody would consider it one of the more glorious episodes in architectural history. The Greek orders always remained curiosities – specimens brought out of a museum. Since the Greeks had never evolved the daring mechanics of style which the Romans had done, since the Greeks never used the arch or the vault or built huge multi-storey buildings, the revived Greek elements tended to be used as cumbersome and costly appendages to modern buildings of otherwise rather negative character. Look at the photograph of the High School at Edinburgh by Thomas Hamilton, built in 1825 – certainly a most spectacular and persuasive Greek Doric performance, beautifully sited on Calton Hill. But I really believe that if all this architecture were taken away the High School as a functioning building would still be there, and it would get a great deal more light. Much the same could be said of the British Museum. Of course, I know this is not quite fair. 'Useless' porticos and 'useless' colonnades are perfectly legitimate means of architectural expression, but when they become a sort of cultural luggage carried by buildings which they screen, cover and adorn, but do not really control, a very dead dead-end has been reached.

Now Sir John Soane, who had one of the most original and explorative minds of the period that saw the Greek Revival, never committed himself to anything of this kind. He always designed his buildings from inside out. He knew his Greek orders very well. He

96

knew his Roman orders even better. He knew his Italians. He had a keen appreciation of Laugier. And knowing all this he was able to go to the root of the matter and make his own statements as to the fundamentals of architecture. Laugier's primitivism – the idea of going back to prehistoric beginnings – certainly appealed to him but he was prepared to go much further than Laugier in actually eliminating all the conventional orders from his practice and inventing a 'primitive' order of his own. You can see it at his Dulwich Art Gallery, which still stands, and of which a drawing, from the Soane Museum, is illustrated in plate 108. Soane's 'order' here is nothing but a brick pier or a brick strip with a stone necking and a stone projection over it, which is a token cornice. He did not share Laugier's hostility to pilasters. Soane's critics made fun of this order by calling it his 'Bœotian' order. There is not a single conventional column or even a conventional moulding in sight. Everything has been abstracted and then rendered back in Soane's own personal interpretation. It is all very original and seems to point to a new freedom for architecture. It seems so to us, but it did not to the generation that followed. When he died, his style died with him and nobody was sorry. The Greek Revival was dying too. Laugier and his ideas were forgotten. It might seem that the story of the classical language of architecture was finished.

But it was not. Whether the story of that language ever was or ever will be finished I do not know. What I have defined as the essentials of classicism penetrated the stylistic chaos of the nineteenth century and became the vital factors in the architectural revolution of the twentieth – the revolution that gave us the architecture we use today.

91

92

93

## The light of reason

Attempts to guide architectural thought along rational lines come with the Age of Enlightenment. **91** The frontispiece of Laugier's *Essai sur l'Architecture*, 1753, shows the 'rustic cabin' of primitive man, 'the model upon which all the magnificences of architecture have been imagined'. **92, 93** Two earlier allusions to the idea of architecture's primitive origins: a diagram by Philibert de l'Orme, 1576, and a 'rustic' column by Bramante in the cloister of S. Ambrogio, Milan. **94** A plate from Sir William Chambers's *Treatise* of 1759 shows the hypothetical evolution of the Doric order from the primitive hut.

94

95, 96 The perfect building, consisting of an organization of single load-bearing columns, was attempted, though not quite achieved, in the interior of the Panthéon, Paris, begun in 1756; it is the first great monument of neo-classicism.

97

## The light of imagination

The Age of Reason was also, paradoxically, the Age of Imagination. **97** Piranesi's Prison Scenes, published about 1744, derive from the Baroque theatre but are also profoundly architectural – romantic studies in rustication. The orders are absent but the raw masonry arches are still evocative of Rome.

100

98

98 Old Newgate Gaol,
London, by George Dance,
1769; the language of
rustication and the dark
vision of Piranesi are
introduced into a building
conceived as a symbol as well
as a punitive stronghold. 99
In the County Hall, London,
by Ralph Knott, 1911, the
spirit of Piranesi gives
monumentality and prestige
to the seat of an
administrative body.

In the middle of the eighteenth century the quest of the primitive led to the investigation of Greek monuments. Considered at first to be crude prototypes of Roman, their formal sophistication and greater 'purity' of profile were soon admitted. **100** Reasonably accurate details of the Parthenon were available from 1784. **101** By 1825, the date of Thomas Hamilton's High School in Edinburgh, the Doric temples of the Acropolis had become favourite models for innumerable public buildings in England and Scotland.

*101*

## Greece reborn

*102*

**102, 103** For the 45-foot high columns of the British Museum, begun in 1844, Sir Robert Smirke availed himself of the published researches of the Society of Dilettanti in Asia Minor. His Ionic capitals are those of the temple of Athene Polias at Priene.

*103*

## Antique simplicity

Simple geometric silhouettes and archaeological purity of detail go together in the
great monuments of late neo-classicism. **104** Schinkel's Altes Museum in Berlin,
1824–28, presents a façade in the form of an open colonnade of nineteen bays,
unmodulated except where the closing piers step quietly into place. The solid
mass of the central hall rises behind in telling contrast. **105** Somewhat analogous in
disposition are the main elements of St George's Hall, Liverpool, begun by
Harvey Lonsdale Elmes in 1838.

104

105

# CHAPTER SIX

## Classical into Modern

During the first half of the twentieth century the architectural habits of the world completely changed. Within that period, and at the heart of the process of change, we can now trace, as a matter of history, the workings of what we conventionally call the Modern Movement in architecture. The Movement had its beginnings in the decade before 1914. It reached its highest pitch of innovating vigour in the late twenties and, after World War II, exploded like a delayed action bomb, filling the huge vacuum the war years had created. Its effects spread and spread until by now there is no corner of the industrialized world in which the thin, high, glossy blocks, the perspectives of concrete posts and the punched window patterns are not typical and familiar.

Such is the architectural revolution of our century – the most radical and universal in world history. In the course of it, questions of architectural form have tended to recede, giving place to questions of technology and industrialization, large-scale planning and mass-production for social needs, questions of building rather than architecture. Where, in all this, is the 'language' of architecture? For the answer we must go to the historic sources of the Modern Movement, which we shall discover in the thought and performance of the personalities who determined its course. We shall have to look at a series of foreshadowings of the Modern, emerging in consecutive traditions stretching back to the eighteenth century and the 'age of enlightenment'.

You will remember that earlier I touched on the architectural philosophy of the Abbé Laugier, the man who set before the world the image of the primitive hut or 'rustic cabin' as the ultimate source of all architectural beauty. This image was rather quaint – it consisted simply of four tree-trunks with branches set across them for beams and more branches for rafters; and it had no walls. As a building of this kind would be quite useless to anybody, however primitive, it may be assumed that it never existed except in Laugier's imagination. It had

91

no more archaeological sanction than Rousseau's Noble Savage (who came on the literary scene a few years later) had anthropological sanction. It was, in fact, a symbolic diagram; and the meaning of it was that behind Rome, behind Greece, there was a *principle* which was, as it were, pure essence of architecture.

There were implications here which I do not think Laugier himself realized and which took a very long time indeed to unfold. If the primitive hut was 'pure' architecture, did that mean that it was a one hundred per cent efficient solution of a specific problem of shelter? Obviously not. Or did it mean that 'pure' architecture was limited to columns, beams and rafters? That does seem to have been in Laugier's mind and to that extent his primitive hut was simply a reduction to the lowest possible terms of the classical temple form – an expression still well within the classical language of architecture. On the other hand it contained the germ of the *rational* (the column merely a cylindrical post, the pediment merely a built-up triangle); it contained, in fact, the germ of an architecture from which all decorative and plastic expressions were removed and which (once the tree-trunks were given a bit of polish) was strictly an affair of solid geometry. But it was still architecture.

Such an architecture did come into being – or very nearly – towards the end of the eighteenth century. It mostly had rather Utopian implications and one of its most astonishing manifestations is in the ideal city conceived, designed, never executed, but published, in 1805, by the French architect Ledoux. This is a dream city for a dream society and contains some projects as surprising in their purpose as their form. Plate 107 is one of them. It is a centre for the sexual instruction of adolescents – a very high-minded affair, let me say – with an elaborate programme which need not concern us here. But look at the geometry of it, a complex but harmonious disposition of solids in beautiful relation to the landscape. Irresistibly one is reminded of the definition of architecture which Le Corbusier wrote in 1921: 'the play of volumes, disposed with masterly and superb exactitude beneath the light'. Le Corbusier also projected an ideal city, his Ville Radieuse, and it is not surprising that in the 1920s an architectural scholar thought it worth writing a book drawing an analogy between the two Utopias – Ledoux's and Le Corbusier's. This is not to say that Le Corbusier was influenced by Ledoux. So far as I know he was not.

Ledoux's passion for seeing buildings as aggregates of simple geometrical shapes was shared by some others of his time and a little later: the German, Karl Friedrich Schinkel, for instance. In his Altes Museum at Berlin the shapes are very simple but enormously effective. They consist mainly of a rectangular mass, one of whose sides is a transparent screen of columns. These are seen against an inner wall, but behind this wall rises, in the middle, the cubic form of the central hall of the Museum. A simple but very powerful three-dimensional combination indeed, beside which the British Museum, for all the splendour of its colonnades, cuts a rather poor figure. For the British Museum is all colonnade – there is not a single architectural clue to the building behind it, which, so far as the onlooker from outside is concerned, might almost as well not be there.

Now, although I have underlined the importance of pure solid
104 geometry in the Ledoux design and in Schinkel's Museum, it will not have escaped you that in both of them architectural orders are present: in the Ledoux design as a Greek portico at one end of the building controlling its main lines and echoed at the other end by a semicircular colonnade; in the Museum, as a spectacular and beautifully detailed colonnade which has great formal importance in the whole design. The language of classical architecture is still very much alive and the orders are still not only present but in control. Although we may seem, here, to be on the threshold of Modern architecture, that threshold was to take a long time to cross. Most of the nineteenth and part of the twentieth centuries stood between.

The nineteenth century was very much concerned – over-concerned we may think – with the historical styles. Classical buildings were continually being built but they always looked back, not merely to Greece and Rome but to nearly every succeeding phase of classical development, using the past as one glorious quarry of
63 ideas. C. R. Cockerell, in his New Ashmolean building at Oxford, which we looked at earlier, wove into his design ornaments from Greek temples, a columnar arrangement from the Roman triumphal arch, a cornice from Vignola and other elements from sources as far apart as Florentine Mannerism and Nicholas Hawksmoor. Similarly,
114 Charles Garnier's Paris Opera House, built twenty years later than the
81 Ashmolean, contains a basic idea by Bramante, the Louvre colonnade – into which is intruded a subsidiary order on Michelangelo's
68 Capitoline principle – together with some parts of the earlier Louvre

108

and a Roman attic storey. Classical designers were, so to speak, circling round the achievements of the past looking for things which could be done again in a different way or in different combinations.

Meanwhile, the lively and progressive thought of the age of Laugier took what we may think a rather odd turning. To Frenchmen, however classically minded, it was never quite possible to ignore the fact that some of the most daring, powerful and ingenious buildings ever built were the medieval cathedrals standing on their own soil. The French never had quite the nostalgic, parochial reverence for Gothic which the English had; they admired it as engineering. And admiring it thus – for the structural economy and completeness represented by a vaulted church – it was perhaps inevitable that they should transfer the idea of a rational architecture from an interest in classical antiquity to an interest in the Middle Ages. Anyway, the greatest French theorist of the nineteeenth century, Eugène Viollet-le-Duc, spent most of his life elucidating Gothic architecture as a completely rational way of building and then issuing, in his lectures, a challenge to the modern world to create a modern architecture out of iron and glass, as well as timber and masonry – an architecture just as economical, as rational, as the Gothic. His challenge was met in various ways. The experimental Art Nouveau of the 1890s contains several attempted answers to the problems he posed. But none of them really worked; they were far-fetched and smelt too much of the studio. The real answers were to come, after all, not from an ingenious and really rather precarious philosophy of Gothic, but from the classical tradition which all Europe had shared with antiquity for so long.

The story of what is still called the 'Modern Movement' in architecture has been written several times and is likely to be rewritten many times more. Here, my only business with that complex and involved piece of history is to show how and to what extent the classical language which has been the subject of this book entered into it, what effect it had and how much of that effect remains. The most direct way of doing this will be to go straight to the work of two great pioneers of the first generation: the German, Peter Behrens, who was born in 1868; and the Frenchman, Auguste Perret, born in 1873.

Peter Behrens, who started as a painter, was one of the leaders of the German arts and crafts movement of the early 1900s. The great electrical combine, A.E.G., appointed him their architect and artistic adviser, and in 1908 commissioned him to design a turbine erection hall for their factory in Berlin. Behrens was faced here with the problem of designing a building for a strictly industrial purpose, but at the same time giving it the 'prestige' character which the company expected of their architect. It was typical of German thought at this time that Behrens should look back to German neo-classicism and the age of Schinkel, whose Berlin Museum we were considering just now. The Turbine Hall is really a neo-classical building designed on the lines of a temple but with all the stylistic signs and symbols left out or changed. You may remember that Sir John Soane was doing something like this more than a hundred years earlier. And in a sense Behrens in 1908 was not much more advanced than Soane (at Dulwich) in 1811. Except for this: Soane was working out his style in traditional and (so far as he could see) unchanging materials; while Behrens had to accept the challenge of structural steel, a material which, if its economic dictatorship was not accepted, would soon put architects out of business. So in the Turbine Hall the classical colonnade is represented by those unmodulated verticals on the flank of the building which are in fact steel stanchions. The temple portico has shrunk into one great window area, under a 'pediment' which is not triangular but multangular to suit the structure of the roof behind it. At the corners are plain wall surfaces with horizontal lines on them which seem to be a vestigial kind of rustication. None of this would 'tell' in quite the splendid way it does if Behrens had not adopted the device of 'battering' – that is to say leaning in – his solid wall in the same leaning plane as the windows along the side. To what extent this device is purely aesthetic I do not know but it gives relief and shadow at the eaves of the roof in just the place where in a temple we should have the relief and shadow of the cornice.

Behrens's Turbine Hall is a great performance but not a kind of performance that could be repeated very often. The challenge of steel had to be more directly and economically met, and it was Walter Gropius, a pupil of Behrens, who took the next step, moving a good deal further from the neo-classical model but without losing aesthetic integrity or, indeed, the sense of classical order and symmetry. The pre-First World War industrial buildings of Gropius as well as those of Behrens are key monuments of the Modern Movement.

Now turn from Behrens and his pupil Gropius to the Frenchman, Auguste Perret. Here was an entirely different kind of designer. Perret had no need, or desire, to look back to the neo-classicism of the early nineteenth century; as a Frenchman he had in his bones, so to speak, the still living tradition of classical design fostered by the École des Beaux-Arts, that school of design whose most obviously representative building is, I suppose, the Paris Opera House. I think if you glance again at the Opera, and then at Perret's Naval Construction *117* Depot, you will see a certain connection. The latter is all in reinforced concrete, totally without enrichment. But it is thought out in terms of 'orders' – a major order starting from the ground and running up to something rather like an architrave and cornice; and the ghost of a secondary order whose entablature belongs just above the heads of the first-floor windows. There is almost as much 'relief' and almost as much variety of rhythm in this building as in the Opera House. Only there are no mouldings and there is no carving.

In those buildings by two masters of the Modern Movement we have two statements regarding the possible interpretation of the classical language in terms of steel (Behrens) and reinforced concrete (Perret). Buildings such as these claimed in their day a new freedom, unrelated to specific orders and yet still closely related to the rhythms and general disposition of classical architecture. There was no reason at all why this kind of diagrammatic classicism should not prevail indefinitely as the medium for new constructions – indeed, plenty of buildings are still being built very close in expression to Perret's work of the 1920s. But it happened otherwise, chiefly through the creative genius of one man, Le Corbusier, the most inventive mind in the architecture of our time and also, in a curious way, one of the most classical minds.

Le Corbusier was born in 1887. In 1908–09 he was for a short time in Perret's office in Paris; in 1910–11 he spent a few months in Germany with Behrens. His first house, built in Switzerland during World War I, showed the influence of these masters, especially of Perret. After the war he turned to painting and was involved, along with Amédée Ozenfant, in a movement they called Purism, whose aim was to bring a mathematical discipline to bear on what they saw as the imminent disintegration of Cubism. In 1920 Le Corbusier started writing – about architecture. His collected articles were made up into a book, published in 1923, the famous *Vers une Architecture, Towards an Architecture*, probably the most widely circulated and influential architectural book of our time.

Now, one way of putting Le Corbusier's architectural achievement in a nutshell would be to say that he completely reversed modern architecture as he found it – he turned it upside-down. He found men like Behrens and Perret subduing the chaos of empirical engineering and industrial building by disciplining it into a classically designed framework. Le Corbusier threw away this framework and let the industrial forms speak their own, often bizarre, language; but he exercised a more formidable and effective control than the token orders of Behrens and Perret could do by the application of what he has called 'tracés régulateurs', lines of control. In doing this, Le Corbusier was reassuming a kind of control which had never been entirely forgotten but which belongs essentially to the Renaissance and was fundamental to the work both of Alberti and of Palladio.

At the base of this kind of control is the conviction that harmonious relationships in architecture can be secured only if the shapes of rooms and the openings in walls and indeed all elements in a building are made to conform with certain ratios which are related continuously to all other ratios in the building. To what extent rational systems of this kind do produce effects which eye and mind can consciously apprehend I am extremely doubtful. I have a feeling that the real point of such systems is simply that their users (who are mostly their authors) need them; that there are types of extremely fertile, inventive minds which need the tough inexorable discipline of such systems to correct and at the same time stimulate invention. And the fate of these systems seems, on the whole, to confirm this; they rarely survive their authors and users and the next man of fertile genius invents his own. That, however, in no way diminishes their importance.

In the first chapter I said that 'the aim of classical architecture has always been to achieve a demonstrable harmony of parts'. Perhaps the word 'demonstrable' should not have been quite so closely linked with 'always'. Nevertheless a demonstrable harmony – one which results from a specific code to which reference can be made – is something which conforms absolutely with the nature of classicism and lies very close to the use of the orders which are in themselves demonstrations of harmonious composition. For Le Corbusier the demonstration of the harmonious was always extremely important. Even his first Perret-style house of 1916 he published with the 'tracés régulateurs' ruled across the elevations. The Purist manifesto ran in

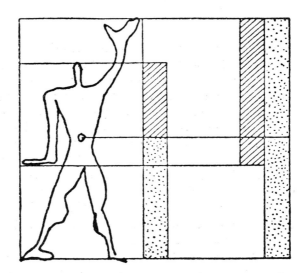

**106** Le Corbusier's diagram to illustrate his concept of the 'Modulor'.

the same direction and the 'tracés' are dealt with – if rather superficially – in a chapter of *Vers une Architecture*. But it was not till the early years of World War II that Le Corbusier created the system which he used in all his later work – the system which he has called the 'Modulor'. 'Modulor' is a word made out of *module* (that is to say, *106* unit of measurement) and *section d'or*, or golden section: that is to say, the division of a line so that the larger part is to the whole line as the smaller part to the larger. The Modulor is a system of space-notation based on this geometrical absolute and constituting a 'gamut' of dimensions. A middle phase of the gamut relates to the dimensions of the human body; the other phases extend it to the minutiae of precision instruments on the one hand and to the scale of vast town-planning enterprises on the other.

Le Corbusier made enormous claims for the Modulor as a system which, if widely adopted, could solve many of the standardization problems of industry and promote harmony throughout our whole physical environment into the bargain. Perhaps it could; but the fact is that, since its publication in 1950, interest in it has rather receded and I am inclined to think that, in this case as in so many others, the real importance of the thing was as part of its author's mental furniture, enabling him to embark on projects as wildly original, for instance, as his chapel at Ronchamp – a building so free in form as to be practically abstract sculpture – always secure in his complete grasp of rational procedure.

So much for the penetration of the classical essence into the Modern Movement. It is now time to answer the question: 'What has happened to the language?' The generally accepted view is that the Modern Movement killed it, and that is not far wrong. One of the most earnestly held beliefs of the Modernists, formulated in Vienna in the lush nineties, was that all ornament was vicious. The architecture of the new age would cast it aside; buildings of the future would appeal to the eye through the harmonious disposition of whatever was necessary for their construction and function – that and no more. This ruthless discipline was immensely important at the time and is still one of the aspects of the Movement which cannot easily be shrugged off as an obsolete puritanical fad. But it did have one devastating side-effect. This was the damage it inflicted on the image of modern architecture in the public mind. If, in the beginning, the mass of people regarded modern architecture as bleak and uninteresting, it was painful to discover that, as the products multiplied, people regarded them as even more bleak and less interesting and, as the years passed, about as attractive as a gorgon's head. The humane intentions of the Movement touched nobody's heart. To all except an informed few, architecture communicated nothing but boredom.

Now, in the 1980s, it has become the fashion to declare the Modern Movement dead. As a serious statement this is arguable, but it is an interesting idea – perhaps the first really inspiring new idea since the Movement was born. It is, anyway, liberating. It means that there may be, once again, some point in discussing architectural language, in trying to define the nature and value of ornament and entering into the whole question of architecture as a vehicle of social meaning. From such speculations the classical language of architecture will never be far absent. The understanding of it will surely remain one of the most potent elements in architectural thought.

## Modern Simplicity

Simplicity of form, seen as an aspect of primitive nobility, pointed very speedily towards architectural radicalism. **107** The naked geometry of Ledoux's 'Oikema' in his ideal city of *c.* 1785 is revolutionary, though he still makes obeisance to archaeology in the porticos. **108** Sir John Soane's personal style dispenses with the grammatical expression of antiquity but provides 'primitive' equivalents in the shape of plain brick pilaster-strips and grooved surfaces, seen here in the Dulwich Art Gallery, 1811, with the founder's mausoleum. **109** Soane's halls at the Bank of England were almost the last word in the reduction of classical concepts to sheer combination of light, surfaces and space: the Colonial Office, 1818.

110

111

112

112

## Neo-classicism continued

Neo-classicism had a long life. The storms of nineteenth-century romanticism passed over without destroying it and the style emerged with all its old literalness and gravity in twentieth-century America. **110** In Munich, Leo von Klenze created the Königsplatz, an uncompromisingly Grecian urban composition consisting of a Propylaeum and museums of painting and sculpture. The Glyptothek seen here was begun in 1816. **111** In France, Henri Labrouste gave a new twist to the story in his Library of Ste Geneviève, 1840–50. The building has no orders but the resources of the classical language are used to render the building not only functional but symbolic of its function; within the stone shell, the structure is mainly of iron, handled with Pompeian elegance. **112** The Lincoln Memorial, Washington, by Henry Bacon, shows neo-classicism still unexhausted in 1917.

117

113

**The Beaux-Arts tradition**

114

115

The École des Beaux-Arts, the dominant centre of architectural education in Europe from 1819 to 1914, promoted an architectural philosophy which spread across the world. This was the philosophy of the *plan*. The horizontal trace of a building was held to be not only the clue to its efficient performance but the generator of its total artistic effect. **113** The plan of Charles Garnier's Opera House, Paris, is not only well contrived but makes a beautiful pattern on paper. **114** The external expression of the Opera is eclectic within the boundaries of Europe's classical tradition: the pavilions of Lescot's Louvre, the Louvre colonnade and Michelangelo's Capitoline Palaces are laid under tribute; ornament is lavish, lush, inventive. **115** Joseph Poelaert's Palace of Justice in Brussels, 1866–83, rises from a plan hardly less accomplished than Garnier's but the exterior expression is a mountain of arrogant and outrageous anomalies – a curious characterization, surely, of the building's purpose.

119

116

117

Innovating masters of the twentieth century have come to terms in one way or another with the classical language, though the terms have invariably meant rigorous exclusion of the orders and their conventional attributes. With the disappearance of the orders, the story of the classical language, as we have defined it, ends. **116** The AEG Turbine Erection Hall, Berlin, an innovating building of 1908 by Peter Behrens, still reflects the temple image, with pediments, colonnades and rustication in paraphrase. **117** Auguste Perret's Naval Construction Depot, 1929, uses the device of major and subsidiary orders, though the 'orders' are never expressed, only implied in the pattern.

120

## Classical into modern

118 The Haus der Kunst at Munich, 1937, represents the Nazi withdrawal from the Modern Movement into a token neo–classicism, negative and heartless. 119 Finally, the Philharmonic Hall of the Lincoln Center, New York, by Max Abramovitz, 1962, is an example of the type of building where a residual feeling for classical rhythm and proportions merges with Modernist sensibility.

118

119

# Glossary

ABACUS. The top part of any capital; as it were a square slab placed on top of the capital to bear the beam (architrave) (pl. 126).

ABUTMENT. The solid mass from which an arch springs.

ACANTHUS. The plant of which a highly conventionalized version decorates the capitals of the Corinthian and Composite orders.

**120** Natural acanthus leaf

**121** Stylized acanthus

**122** Aedicule

ACROTERIA. Small pedestals (originally for sculpture but often seen without) at the extremities and apex of a pediment (pl. 131).

AEDICULE. The architectural frame of an opening, consisting usually of two columns supporting an entablature and pediment.

AMPHIPROSTYLE. See TEMPLE.

ANTA. Equivalent to PILASTER but mostly applied to Greek architecture, where the anta capital is different from that of the columns accompanying it. A portico is said to be *in antis* when the end walls project flush with the columns (see pl. 132).

ARAEOSTYLE. See INTERCOLUMNIATION.

ARCHITRAVE. The lowest of the three primary divisions of the ENTABLATURE. The word is loosely applied to any moulding round a door or window and such mouldings do, in fact, most frequently borrow the profile of the architrave in the strict sense (pl. 124).

ARCHITRAVE-CORNICE. An entablature from which the frieze is elided.

ARCHIVOLT. An architrave moulding when it follows the line of an arch.

ASTRAGAL. A small moulding of circular profile (pl. 124).

ATTIC BASE. See BASE.

ATTIC STOREY. A storey placed over the main entablature of a building and in strictly architectural relation to it (as e.g. in some triumphal arches).

BASE (of a column). There are three main varieties. *1*, The Attic base, the commonest, which is found with all orders except the Tuscan; it consists of two tori separated by a scotia and fillets. *2*, The Tuscan base, consisting simply of a torus and fillet. *3*, A type consisting of two scotiae separated by two astragals with a torus above and a torus below. This, with variations of it, is applicable to the Ionic, Corinthian and Composite (pl. 125).

BEAD-AND-REEL. See ENRICHMENTS.

BED MOULDINGS. The mouldings between the corona (q.v.) and the frieze (q.v.) in any entablature (pl. 124).

**123** Bukranium

BUKRANIA. Carved representations of ox skulls, often found in the metopes of the Doric frieze.

123

CAPITAL (of a column). Each of the five orders has its appropriate capital. Those of the Tuscan and (Roman) Doric are much alike, consisting mainly of abacus, ovolo and, further down, an astragal; the Doric has more multiplicity of small mouldings than the Tuscan. The Ionic is distinguished by *volutes*. These are the coiled ends of an element inserted between the abacus and the ovolo. Sometimes, however, the volutes spring separately from the ovolo. The Corinthian capital is decorated with two ranks of acanthus leaves, while fern-like stems reach out to the corners of the abacus. The Composite capital combines Corinthian leaves with Ionic volutes.

CARYATIDES. Female figures supporting an entablature. The most famous example is at the Erectheum, Athens, where Vitruvius improbably supposed the figures to represent Carian captives, hence the generic name.

CAVETTO. A hollow moulding, whose profile is usually a quarter of a circle (pl. 125).

COLOSSAL ORDER. Any order whose columns extend from the ground through several storeys.

COMPOSITE ORDER. This order, which combines features of the Ionic with the Corinthian, is not described by Vitruvius and was probably evolved after his time. It was first identified by Alberti (*c.* 1450) and first figured by Serlio as the fifth and most elaborate of the five orders.

CONSOLE. A bracket in the form of an S-shaped scroll, with one end broader than the other. A console has many applications, either vertical (e.g. against a wall to carry a bust) or horizontal (as the visible part of a cantilever supporting a gallery). Keystones of arches are often modelled as consoles.

CORINTHIAN ORDER. This order was an Athenian invention of the 5th century BC but in early examples is only differentiated from the Ionic by its leaf-enfurled capital. Even Vitruvius, in the 1st century AD, described only the capital 'because the Corinthian order has not separate rules for the cornices and other ornaments'. However, in later Roman practice the Corinthian entablature crystallized as something quite distinct. The original design of the capital is attributed by Vitruvius to the sculptor Callimachus who, he says, was inspired by the sight of a basket of toys placed, with a stone slab for protection (the abacus), on the grave of a Corinthian girl and around which wild acanthus had grown. The Corinthian order, as employed from the 16th century onwards, is based on Roman examples, notably the temples of Vespasian and Castor and Pollux in the Forum.

fillet
cyma recta
cyma reversa
corona
modillions
ovolo (egg + dart)
dentils
cyma reversa
astragal (bead + reel)

Cornice

Frieze

fillet
cyma reversa
astragal
fascia
cyma reversa
fascia
astragal
fascia

Architrave

column shaft

fluting

torus
scotia
torus
cyma reversa
astragal
cyma recta

astragal

Base

plinth
fascia
cavetto

dado or die

Pedestal

cavetto
astragal

torus

plinth

**124, 125** The Corinthian order: entablature and base

CORNICE. The uppermost of the three primary divisions of the
ENTABLATURE (q.v.). The word is loosely applied to almost any
horizontal moulding forming a main decorative feature, especially to a
moulding at the junction of walls and ceiling in a room. Such mouldings
do, traditionally, follow the profiles of cornices in the strict sense (pl. 124).

125

CORONA. The part of a cornice forming a sudden projection over the bed-moulding (q.v.).

CYMA RECTA. A moulding which is concave in its upper part and convex below (pl. 124).

CYMA REVERSA. A moulding which is convex in its upper part and concave below (pl. 124).

DECASTYLE. See PORTICO.

DENTILS. Small closely spaced blocks forming one of the members of a cornice in the Ionic, Corinthian, Composite and, more rarely, Doric orders (pl. 124).

DIASTYLE. See INTERCOLUMNIATION.

DIPTERAL. See TEMPLE.

DISTYLE IN ANTIS. A disposition comprising two columns between pilasters or antae.

DODECASTYLE. See PORTICO.

**126** The Doric order

DORIC ORDER. The Greek Doric and Roman Doric both have, ultimately, a Greek origin but they developed in different ways. They have in common (1) the presence of triglyphs in the frieze, with mutules and guttae on the soffit of the corona and (2) the fact that the capital consists of little more than an abacus supported by a moulding or mouldings. The Greek order has no base, nor is a base prescribed by Vitruvius though in practice the Roman Doric nearly always has a base, the Greek never. As full knowledge and appreciation of the Greek order was only regained in the late 18th century, its appearance in the modern world before *c*. 1800 is rare.

ECHINUS (pl. 126). See OVOLO.

EGG-AND-DART. See ENRICHMENTS.

**127** Enrichments: egg-and-dart, bead-and-reel, water-leaf

ENRICHMENTS. Certain standard types of carved enrichment are appropriate to certain standard profiles. Thus, the ovolo is enriched with *egg-and-dart*, the cyma reversa with *water-leaf*, the bead or astragal with *bead-and-reel*. For the cyma recta, less frequently enriched, laurel leaves or honey-suckle are appropriate. In other elements of the order there is a wide margin of choice in enrichment.

ENTABLATURE. The whole assemblage of parts supported by the column. The three primary divisions are ARCHITRAVE, FRIEZE and CORNICE. Of these, only the architrave and cornice are subdivided.

ENTASIS. The swelling of a column. All classical columns are broader at the base than at the capital. The diminution often begins one-third of the way up the column and thereafter takes the form of a curve whose setting-out is prescribed in various ways.

EUSTYLE. See INTERCOLUMNIATION.

FASCIA. A plain horizontal band. A common form of architrave consists of two or three fasciae each slightly oversailing the one below and perhaps separated from it by a narrow moulding (pl. 124).

FILLET. A narrow horizontal strip separating the larger curved mouldings in a cornice or base (pl. 124).

FLUTING. Vertical channels, of rounded section, cut in the shafts of columns. Never found in the Tuscan and optional in the other orders. Sometimes the lower flutings are filled with solid cylindrical pieces; they are then described as *cabled* flutings.

127

FRIEZE. The middle of the three primary divisions of the ENTABLATURE. In essence the frieze is a plain horizontal band between the elaborately shelving cornice above and the architrave (which may or may not be divided into fasciae) below. But the Doric frieze usually contains triglyphs; while in the Ionic, Corinthian and Composite orders the frieze is often appropriated to figure-sculpture (pl. 124).

GUTTAE. Small conical pieces carved on the architrave below the taenia under each triglyph in the Doric order. They evidently represent wooden pegs and thus originate, as does the triglyph, in the timber prototypes of the Doric (pl. 126).

HEXASTYLE. See PORTICO.

IMPOST. The moulding of a pier at the springing of an arch.

**128** Intercolumniation

⌊..Eustyle..⌋.Diastyle___⌋_____Araeostyle___⌋

INTERCOLUMNIATION. The distance, measured in diameters, between two columns. The types named by Vitruvius, with the ratios later assigned to them, are as follows: *Pycnostyle*, $1\frac{1}{2}$ D; *Systyle*, 2 D; *Eustyle*, $2\frac{1}{4}$ D; *Diastyle*, 3 D; *Araeostyle*, 4 D. Other intercolumniations are found in the Doric order where spacing is necessarily controlled by the triglyph-metope rhythm in the frieze. Eustyle intercolumniation is the most common.

IONIC ORDER. This order, which originated in Asia Minor about the middle of the 6th century BC, is distinguished in Roman examples by two main characteristics: *1*, the voluted capital; *2*, the presence of dentils in the cornice. Vitruvius gives a minute description of the order.

METOPE. The square space between two triglyphs in the frieze of the Doric order. Often left plain but sometimes decorated with bukrania, trophies or other ornaments (pl. 126).

MODILION. An ornament in the cornice of the Corinthian and Composite orders. A modilion is a diminutive CONSOLE or scrolled bracket and the modilions in a cornice give the appearance of supporting the corona. They are spaced so as to allow a square sinking in the soffit between each pair (pl. 124).

MODULE. The relative sizes of all parts of an order are traditionally given in Modules, a Module being half the diameter of the column just above its moulded base. The Module is divided into thirty minutes. Sometimes the diameter itself is called the Module, in which case it contains sixty minutes.

MUTULE. A square block carved on the soffit of the corona in the Doric order immediately over each triglyph (pl. 126). See TRIGLYPH.

OCTASTYLE. See PORTICO.

ORDER. An order is the total assemblage of parts comprising the column and its appropriate entablature. The primary divisions of the column are base, shaft and capital. The primary divisions of the entablature are architrave, frieze and cornice. A pedestal under the column is not an essential part of the order but appropriate pedestals are given by the theorists from Serlio onwards.

OVOLO. A convex moulding whose profile is usually a quarter of a circle (pl. 124).

PALLADIAN MOTIF. The name given by the French (motif Palladio) to the combination of arch and columns conspicuously illustrated in Palladio's

**129** Palladian motif

Basilica at Vicenza. In principle the arrangement consists of an opening where an arch stands over columns whose entablatures are the lintels of narrower side openings (see VENETIAN WINDOW). In Palladio's Basilica this triple opening is framed in the bays formed by a superior order and it is to this system that the term 'Palladian Motif' should be confined.

PEDESTAL. A substructure under a column (pl. 125). See ORDER.

PEDIMENT. The triangular space created by the sloping eaves and horizontal cornice line of a gabled temple or other classical building. The word appears to be an alteration of *periment*, the word used in 16th-century English accounts and perhaps deriving from French *parement*, facing. Pediments do not always express the end of a roof but are often used ornamentally, even on a large scale. On a miniature scale they commonly surmount door and window openings. There are many varieties and distortions of the pediment, e.g. the pediment with a curved (segmental) instead of pointed top, and the 'broken pediment' whose sloping sides are returned before reaching the apex (pl. 131).

PERIPTERAL. See TEMPLE.

PERISTYLE. A continuous colonnade surrounding a temple or court.

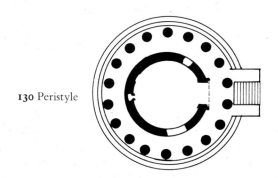

**130** Peristyle

PIER. The solids between door, window or other openings. Piers are invariably part of the carrying structure of a building. They may or may not be combined or overlaid with pilasters, half columns, three-quarter columns, etc.

PILASTER. The representation in relief of a column against a wall. The pilaster is sometimes considered as the visible part of a square column built into the wall. Pilasters are necessarily ornamental. They have a quasi-structural function, however, when acting as *responds*, i.e. as the thickening of a wall opposite a column whose entablature carries over to the wall.

PILLAR. A word in common use which has no specific meaning in the context of classical architecture.

PLINTH. The square solid under the base of a column or pedestal (pl. 125).

PODIUM. A structure, usually massive, providing a platform on which a classical building is placed.

**131** Octastyle portico

PORTICO. A place for walking under shelter. The word is usually applied to the columned projection before the entrance to a temple or similar building. Porticos of this kind are described according to the number of frontal columns, viz. *Tetrastyle* (4), *Hexastyle* (6), *Octastyle* (8), *Decastyle* (10) and *Dodecastyle* (12). Where there are only two columns between pilasters or antae the expression used is *Distyle in Antis*.

PROSTYLE. See TEMPLE.

PSEUDODIPTERAL. See TEMPLE.

PSEUDOPERIPTERAL. See TEMPLE.

PYCNOSTYLE. See INTERCOLUMNIATION.

QUOINS. Usually the external angles of buildings, especially when these are emphasized by rustication.

131

RUSTICATION. Masonry (or an imitation thereof) where the joints between the stones are deliberately emphasized by sinkings or where the stones are left rough or worked in such a way as to afford a striking textural effect.

SCOTIA. A hollow moulding, most often seen between the tori in bases of columns (pl. 125).

SHAFT. That part of a column which is between the base and the capital.

SOFFIT. The under-side of any architectural element, e.g. a corona, or an architrave where it does not rest on columns.

STYLOBATE. The steps under a portico or colonnade (pl. 131).

SYSTYLE. See INTERCOLUMNIATION.

TAENIA. The narrow projecting band between architrave and frieze in the Doric order (pl. 126).

TEMPLE. The disposition of columns around temples has given rise to the following nomenclature. *Prostyle:* a temple with a portico in front only; *Amphiprostyle:* with porticos at front and rear; *Peripteral:* with porticos connected by open colonnades along the sides; *Pseudoperipteral:* with porticos connected only by pilasters or columns in relief; *Dipteral:* with porticos connected by double ranges of columns along the sides; *Pseudodipteral:* with the same arrangement as regards spacing, but the inner ranges of columns omitted.

**132** Temple with columns *in antis*

**133** Prostyle temple

**134** Amphiprostyle temple

**136** Dipteral temple      **138** Pseudodipteral temple

**135** Peripteral temple      **137** Pseudoperipteral temple

TETRASTYLE. See PORTICO.

TORUS. A moulding of semicircular profile used in the bases of columns (pl. 125).

TRIGLYPH. A feature of the frieze of the Doric order, consisting of a vertical element with two sunk vertical channels and two half-channels at the edges. The triglyph is related to the mutule above and to the guttae below. The whole system is a paraphrase in masonry of features deriving from timber construction (pl. 126).

TUSCAN ORDER. This order derives from an ancient type of Etruscan temple and, as Vitruvius describes it, is of primitive character with wide spaces between the columns, necessarily involving timber beams. The 16th-century theorists regarded it as proto-Doric and the crudest and most massive of the five orders.

**139** Venetian window

VENETIAN WINDOW. A triple opening in which the wider central opening is closed by an arch while the side openings have lintels. Not characteristically Venetian but used by Bramante and Raphael, later by Scamozzi, and adopted by Inigo Jones. In English 18th-century practice it was common. A variant in which an outer relieving arch, concentric with the inner arch, extends over all three openings, was derived by Lord Burlington from a drawing by Palladio and used in several of his works and after him by English architects till far into the 19th century.

VOLUTE. See CAPITAL.

VOUSSOIR. A block of stone, or other material, which is one of a series constituting an arch.

WATER-LEAF. See ENRICHMENTS.

# Notes on the Literature of Classical Architecture

Classical architecture has always, even in ancient times, depended on precedents and, therefore, on written treatises. Vitruvius himself declared his indebtedness to ancient authors and the classicism of the modern world has been to a great extent dependent on Vitruvius. Editions of his work, therefore, take precedence in any review of the literature of classical architecture. Next to Vitruvius, the treatises of 16th-century Italy are of the greatest consequence; they are followed by the treatises of other nations which invariably refer back both to Vitruvius and to the Italians. The following lists are highly selective and include only the best-known and most representative treatises of the main European countries.

## Vitruvius

Vitruvius wrote his treatise, *De Architectura*, in the first quarter of the 1st century AD. He was the only Roman writer on architecture whose work survived to be copied and recopied through the Middle Ages. The oldest existing manuscript is in the British Museum (Harl. 2767); it belongs to the 8th century and was probably written at Jarrow. There are sixteen later medieval manuscripts in various European libraries. The first printed text appeared in Rome about 1486. The next editions were those of Fra Giocondo (Florence, 1522) and Philander (Rome, 1544). Of great importance were the illustrated translations by Cesariano (Como, 1521) and Daniele Barbaro (Venice, 1567; with illustrations by Palladio). From the 16th century onwards there are translations, paraphrases and commentaries in nearly every European language. A good modern text translation is that by Frank Granger for the Loeb Classical Library (Heinemann, 1931; 2nd ed. 1944–56. 2 vols).

## Italian Treatises

LEON BATTISTA ALBERTI (1404–1472), *De Re Aedificatoria*. Presented in MS. to Pope Nicholas V, 1452. First printed (in Latin) in Florence, 1485. The first Italian translation appeared in Venice in 1546 and the first illustrated edition in 1550. A French translation by Jean Martin followed in 1553. In England, Giacomo Leoni's translation (*Ten Books on Architecture*) appeared in 1726. A reduced facsimile of this (with introduction and notes by J. Rykwert) was published in 1955.

Alberti's treatise, although making exhaustive use of Vitruvius, is a great original work setting forth the principles of architecture in the light of the author's own philosophy and of his analysis of Roman buildings. It profoundly influenced all subsequent Italian theory.

SEBASTIANO SERLIO (1475–1552), published in his lifetime six books of architecture, all richly illustrated. In 1566, the first five were assembled as a single treatise, though not in the order they were written. The subjects of these five are (with original publication dates): 1, *Geometry* (1545); 2, *Perspective* (1545); 3, *Antiquities* (1537); 4, *The Orders* (1540); 5, *Churches* (1547). A sixth book called *Libro Estraordinario*, containing designs for arches and gateways, was published in 1551 and republished in 1566. Two posthumous books (7 and 8) made up from Serlio's drawings were published with the others at Frankfurt in 1575. The first, and only, English edition was published in 1611.

Serlio's work is both a textbook and a treasury of designs. It became the standard authority on architecture and the most popular source-book throughout Europe in the later 16th and 17th centuries, Serlio's versions of the five orders being at the root of most expositions outside Italy, till they were superseded by Vignola and Palladio.

GIACOMO BAROZZI DA VIGNOLA (1507–1573), *Regola delli Cinque Ordini d'Architettura*, 1562. A set of fine engravings on copper of versions of the five orders, based on Roman examples and with reference to Vitruvius. More refined and scholarly than Serlio. No text – only introduction and notes, but the book includes a number of Vignola's own designs. Many later editions, mostly Italian and French. First English edition in 1669.

ANDREA PALLADIO (1508–1580), *I Quattro Libri dell'Architettura*, Venice, 1570. The four books deal respectively with: 1, *The Orders*, 2, *Domestic Buildings* (including Palladio's own palaces and villas), 3, *Public Buildings* (mostly Roman, but including Palladio's Basilica at Vicenza) and 4, *Temples* (Roman). Palladio's orders are as refined as Vignola's. His illustrations of Roman antiquities are a great advance on Serlio's – they were, in fact, not superseded as records till Desgodetz's work of 1682. The inclusion of Palladio's own designs resulted in his recognition throughout Europe, but especially in England, as the greatest modern interpreter of classical architecture. English editions, 1663, 1715, 1736 and 1738.

VINCENZO SCAMOZZI (1552–1616), *Dell' Idea dell'Architettura Universale*, Venice, 1615. A massive work, owing much to Palladio, but designed to promote a pure, academic classicism which belongs in spirit to the 18th century rather than to the 17th.

## French Treatises

PHILIBERT DE L'ORME (*c.* 1510–1570), *Architecture*, Paris, 1567. A work of great originality, combining thought deriving from medieval French tradition with sensitive and scholarly observation of Roman architecture.

ROLAND FRÉART (d. 1676), *Parallèle de l'Architecture Antique et de la Moderne*, Paris, 1650. A detailed critical review by a scholar, of all the established versions of the orders, ancient and modern. English edition by John Evelyn, 1664.

CLAUDE PERRAULT (1613–1688), *Ordonnances des Cinq Espèces de Colonne*, Paris, 1676. A critical dissertation on the orders with Perrault's own preferred versions. Perrault's translation of Vitruvius (Paris, 1684), with copious commentary, ranks as a treatise of major importance.

G.L. DE CORDEMOY (1651–1722), *Nouveau Traité de Toute l'Architecture*, 1706. Ostensibly concerned mostly with the orders but actually a revolutionary 'anti-Baroque' statement demanding a new purity of conception in design.

M.A. LAUGIER (1713–1769), *Essai sur l'Architecture*, Paris, 1753. Deriving mainly from Cordemoy, Laugier carries the latter's rationalism to extremes.

The above are only a few of the many French treatises. A type of great importance in the 18th and 19th centuries was that introduced by FRANÇOIS BLONDEL (1679–1719), who published his Academy lectures as *Cours d'Architecture* (Paris 1675). Other treatises based on lecture courses but encyclopaedic in character are those of A.C. D'AVILER (Paris, 1691) and JACQUES FRANÇOIS BLONDEL (Paris, 1771–1777). The *Leçons* of J.N.L. DURAND (Paris, 1801–1805 and later) reflect the severe rationalism deriving from Laugier.

## German and Flemish Treatises

HANS BLUM, *Quinque Columnarum exacta descriptio atque delineatio*, Zurich, 1550. An exposition of the orders based on Serlio, often republished. First English edition, 1608.

VREDEMAN DE VRIES (1527–1604), *Architectura*, Antwerp, 1577 (many later eds.). The orders, based on Serlio but elaborated and enriched.

WENDEL DIETTERLIN (c. 1550–1599), *Architectura*, Nuremberg, 1594–1598. Extravaganzas on the orders.

## English Treatises

JOHN SHUTE (d. 1563), *The First and Chief Groundes of Architecture*, London, 1563 (Facsimile, with introd. by L. Weaver, 1912). The orders, after Serlio, with variations.

JAMES GIBBS (1682–1754), *Rules for Drawing the Several Parts of Architecture*, London, 1732. An admirably clear textbook rather than a treatise.

ISAAC WARE (d. 1766), *The Complete Body of Architecture*, London, 1756. An encyclopaedic work representative of the Palladian movement.

SIR WILLIAM CHAMBERS (1723–1796), *A Treatise on Civil Architecture*, London, 1759. Republished in 1791 as *A Treatise on the Decorative Part of Civil Architecture* and again in 1825 (ed. Joseph Gwilt). A historical and critical work of great refinement.

## Modern Historical Works in English

*For the architecture of the ancient world:*

A.W. LAWRENCE, *Greek Architecture* (Pelican History of Art). Penguin Books, 1957.

D.S. ROBERTSON, *Handbook of Greek and Roman Architecture*, Cambridge University Press, 1929. 2nd ed., 1943.

R.E.M. WHEELER, *Roman Art and Architecture*, Thames and Hudson, 1964.

A. BOËTHIUS and J.B. WARD-PERKINS, *Etruscan and Roman Architecture* (Pelican History of Art). Penguin Books, 1970.

*For the history of architecture since the Renaissance:*

N. PEVSNER, *An Outline of European Architecture*, Penguin Books, 7th ed., 1963. The post-Renaissance chapters give an admirable general perspective, while the bibliography includes important foreign books not listed here.

L.H. HEYDENREICH and W. LOTZ, *Architecture in Italy 1400–1600* (Pelican History of Art). Penguin Books, 1974.

R. WITTKOWER, *Architectural Principles in the Age of Humanism*, Warburg Inst., Univ. of London, 1949. Tiranti, 2nd ed., 1952.

R. WITTKOWER, *Art and Architecture in Italy 1600–1750* (Pelican History of Art). Penguin Books, 1958.

A. BLUNT, *Art and Architecture in France, 1500–1700* (Pelican History of Art). Penguin Books, 1953.

ALAN BRAHAM, *Architecture of the French Enlightenment*, Thames and Hudson, 1980.

J. SUMMERSON, *Architecture in Britain, 1530–1830* (Pelican History of Art). Penguin Books, 1953. 4th ed., 1963.

E. KAUFMANN, *Architecture in the Age of Reason*, Harvard University Press, 1955; Oxford University Press, 1955.

H.R. HITCHCOCK, *Architecture: 19th and 20th centuries* (Pelican History of Art). Penguin Books, 1958.

J. JOEDICKE, *A History of Modern Architecture* (trans. J.C. Palmes), Architectural Press, 1959.

The quotation from Lutyens on p. 27 is from CHRISTOPHER HUSSEY, *The Life of Sir Edwin Lutyens* (1950), p. 133.

# Sources of Illustrations

PHOTOGRAPHS

Albertina, Vienna: 50; Alinari: 19, 32, 40, 55, 66, 78, 79, 87; Anderson: 20, 21, 41, 59, 72, 73, 74, 77; Archives Photographiques: 15, 81, 111; B.T. Batsford: 98; Bazzecchi, Florence: 22; Osvaldo Böhm: 36; British Architectural Library, London: 27; British Architectural Library, Drawings Collection, London: 57; British Museum, London: 82; Brogi: 13, 67; *Country Life*: 47; Courtauld Institute of Art, London: 54; Charles Phelps Cushing: 26; Department of the Environment: 43; Fototeca Unione, Rome: 24; Gabinetto Fotografico Nazionale, Rome: 18, 28; Ewing Galloway: 112; Giraudon: 8, 9, 23, 75; Greater London Council: 99; Hirmer Fotoarchiv: 88, 100; M. Hürlimann: 33; A.F. Kersting: 12, 14, 34, 38, 45, 63, 80, 85, 90, 95, 96, 101, 105, 110, 118; E. Kidder-Smith: 84; Lincoln Center: 119; Roland Liot: 117; I. Mackenzie-Kerr: 29; Mansell: 93; Bildarchiv Foto Marburg: 76, 89, 106; Mas: 52; Georgina Masson: 42, 48, 60; Leonard von Matt: 58; National Monuments Record: 11, 69; Willy Rizzo: 31; N.D. Roger-Viollet: 114; Jean Roubier: 68; Oscar Savio: 37; Alistair Service: 64; Edwin Smith: 35, 49, 83, 86; Trustees of Sir John Soane's Museum, London: 108, 109, 140; Dr Franz Stoedtner: 115, 116; Eileen Tweedy: 65, 103; Soprintendenza ai Monumenti, Venice: 39; University of Virginia, Charlottesville: 30; Virginia State Library: 10.

REPRODUCTIONS FROM BOOKS:

Fancesco Borromini, *Opera*, Rome 1720: 6; Richard Boyle, Earl of Burlington, *Baths of the Romans*, London 1730: 25; William Chambers, *A Treatise on Civil Architecture*, London 1759: 94; R. Chandler, *Ionian Antiquities*, published for the Dilettanti Society, London 1769: 102; A. Desgodetz, *Les Edifices Antiques de Rome*, Paris 1682: 16; Wendel Dietterlin, *Architecture*, Nuremberg 1598: 71; R. Fréart, *Parallèl de l'architecture*, Paris 1650: 7; M.A. Laugier, *Essai sur l'architecture*, Paris 1753: 91; Le Corbusier, *Le Modulor*, 1948: 106; C.N. Ledoux, *L'architecture considerée sous la rapport de l'art des moeurs et de la legislation*, Paris 1804: 107; Philibert de l'Orme, *Le premier tome de l'architecture*, Paris 1568: 5, 92; A. Palladio, *I Quattro Libri dell'Architettura*, (Venice 1570) 1601 edition: 44; A. Palladio, *I Quattro Libri dell'Architettura*, English edition 1738: 46; C. Perrault, *Ordonnances des Cinq Espèces de Colonne*, Paris 1683: 4; G.B. Piranesi, *Vedute di Roma*, Rome c. 1748: 27; G.B. Piranesi, *Prima Parte di Architetture e Prospettive*, Rome 1743: 97; A.E. Richardson, *Monumental Classic Architecture in Great Britain and Ireland*, London 1914: 62; F. Ruggieri, *Studio d'Architettura Civile*, Florence 1722–28: 53; V. Scamozzi, *L'idea dell'Architettura Universale*, Venice 1615: 3; K.F. Schinkel, *Sammlung Architektonischer Entwürfe*, Berlin 1819–40: 104; S. Serlio *Il Libro Primo (-Quinto) d'Architettura*, 1554: 1, 51; G. Barozzi da Vignola, *Regola delli Cinque Ordini d'Architettura*, 1607: 2, 17, 61; J. Vredeman de Vries, *Architectura*, 1563: 70. ENGRAVINGS by: E. Dupérac, 56; A. Lafreri, 37; after J. Maurer, 82.

# Index

Numbers in **bold** type refer to plate numbers

143